Homeschooling
for the Rest of Us

Books by
Sonya Haskins
FROM BETHANY HOUSE PUBLISHERS

The Homeschooler's Book of Lists
Homeschooling for the Rest of Us

Homeschooling for the Rest of Us

**How Your One-of-a-Kind Family
Can Make Homeschooling and
Real Life Work**

Sonya Haskins

BETHANYHOUSE
Minneapolis, Minnesota

Published by Bethany House Publishers
11400 Hampshire Avenue South
Bloomington, Minnesota 55438

Bethany House Publishers is a division of
Baker Publishing Group, Grand Rapids, Michigan.

Printed in the United States of America

Library of Congress Cataloging-in-Publication Data

Haskins, Sonya A.
  Homeschooling for the rest of us : how your one-of-a-kind family can make homeschooling and real life work / Sonya Haskins.
     p.   cm.
  Summary: "Presents advice for overcoming stress, unrealistic expections, and other challenges faced by homeschooling families. Intended for new and experienced homeschoolers. Applicable to a variety of teaching methods"—Provided by publisher.
  ISBN 978-0-7642-0739-6 (pbk. : alk. paper)
  1. Home schooling. I. Title.
  LC40.H378   2010
  371.04'2—dc22
                                                                2009040691

For Sandy Howard
and
For Angie Tyson

"A true friend is someone who thinks you are a good egg even though he knows that you are slightly cracked."
—Bernard Meltzer

About the Author

Sonya Haskins and her family see each day as an adventure in learning. A homeschooling consultant and mom of five children, ages six to thirteen, she is also the author of *The Homeschooler's Book of Lists* and six regional history books. Sonya is active in national, state, and local homeschool activities; however, most of her time is divided between her family and ministering to other homeschool families through writing, speaking engagements, or individual consultations.

Sonya's articles have appeared online and in *Homeschooling Today, Educational Dealer, Pastor's Family, Decision, Guideposts for Teens, The Upper Room,* and other publications.

Although it is apparent in her writings that she advocates personalized teaching styles that fit individual families, Sonya follows a relaxed homeschool method in her own home. She provides the educational tools, opportunities, and encouragement that create an environment conducive to learning, and her children are responsible for taking advantage of those resources. Sonya and her husband and children live in the beautiful mountains of northeast Tennessee.

If you are interested in reading more about relaxed homeschooling or just about anything related to home education, visit Sonya's Web site at *www.thehomeschooladvocate.com.* If you are a homeschool family (or you're thinking about homeschooling) and have questions, you can contact her at *sonya@sonyahaskins.com.*

Acknowledgments

Thank you to everyone who prayed for me while I wrote this book. Without those prayers, it would not have been finished.

I'd also like to thank Jeff Braun, my editor. He is great to work with, as is all the staff at Bethany House, including the team who thought of the fabulous title for this book!

During the final weeks of finishing a book, the burden of caring for our home, children, and homeschooling falls primarily on my husband. Chris has always been very supportive of my writing, and I am grateful for this.

When I'm writing I spend a lot of time at Fresh Deli (formerly Poor Richard's Uptown) and Golden Corral in Johnson City, Tennessee. I appreciate the managers, waitresses, and staff allowing me to take up a table when I need a place to write.

Thanks also to my children, Steven and Liesl Huhn, Audrey Headrick, Stan and Kara Sanders, Art and Bonnie Joyce, the Nerrin family, Mary Tucker, Vivian Gamble, Cathy Hawkins, Kimberly Prillhart, Wendy Owens, Lori Keck, Mary Simonsen, Melinda Chapman, Toni Stacy, Ruth Jackson, Mary Gilbert, Rebecca Moreland, Tammy McFaddin, and members of the Tri-Cities Homeschool Digest and also my church (Johnson City Alliance Church), as well as the many others who provided moral support and encouragement throughout the development of this book.

Thank you!

Contents

Chapter 1

That's Homeschooling . . . Right?

Matching outfits, polite toddlers, award-winning students, fifteen-passenger vans, and family Web sites.

It is easy to think homeschooling families are "perfect," but what if you want to homeschool and your family isn't perfect? What if you're already homeschooling and there are days when you aren't sure if what you did actually qualifies as "educational hours" under your state's requirements? A typical day includes a trip to the store in the same car you had when you met your husband in college, and you realize just as you enter the store that one of your children isn't wearing shoes, and then your toddler has a meltdown the moment you run into your critical neighbor in the produce aisle. If your family did have a Web site, it would look more like homeschooling with *The Three Stooges* than *Leave It to Beaver*.

With the pressures placed on homeschoolers to be perfect and the commitment required to successfully teach a child at home, it's no wonder many families throw in the towel before they have an opportunity to develop their own rhythm or experience the benefits of teaching at home.

Frequently, information for homeschoolers or those considering homeschooling concentrates on perfect families, perfect children, perfect curricula, and even perfect schedules. Or at least they appear perfect. Although this type of material is appealing (who doesn't want to be perfect?), it's impractical for the average household. Even if perfection could be achieved, what's the cost to your sanity?

Magazines tell homeschoolers to relax, yet they consistently have photos of families in hand-made matching clothes that the sixteen-year-old daughter designed when she wasn't volunteering at the local hospice center.

> We are a new home-school family. The first half of the year was difficult. I didn't know what kind of a homeschooler I was trying to be and I was impatient to learn the "right way of homeschooling" for my children. There is often no "right way," but just a constant search for a better way.
>
> —Tamiko C.,
> British Columbia

Books present one extreme viewpoint or another: If people don't homeschool, it's a sin. Anyone interested in homeschooling for religious reasons is a fanatic. If you simply follow the suggestions in the book, it will fix all your problems.

Moreover, as society places pressure on homeschoolers to be perfect, media reports can perpetuate myths about how homeschooling is harmful for children. They tell stories of homeschooled students who have been locked away from society and are abused. Yet many of these stories are unfounded and involve truancy cases rather than actual homeschoolers. Homeschoolers are also portrayed as ultra-intelligent freaks that have been drilled by obsessive parents living out their academic-achievement fantasies through their children.

At the other end of the spectrum, we see on TV how the Duggars, a homeschooling family with eighteen children (at last count), live an idealistic, debt-free, non-voice-raising, godly child-training life in Arkansas. I have great respect for any family who seems to have it all together, but I would wager that most homeschooling families are taking baby steps toward achieving their goals.

So where does this leave the rest of us?

For the nearly three million homeschoolers in the United States and the millions more worldwide, this leaves the majority of us in the middle of perfectly normal families trying to make sense of the world, find joy in the midst of chaos, and educate our children.

In the following chapters you will discover that there is no perfect homeschooling family, child, curriculum, schedule, or disciplinary method. Hopefully you will not feel judged, chastised, or condemned while reading this book. My husband and I have learned many lessons homeschooling our five children, now ages six to thirteen, and parenting over fifty foster children from newborn through age eighteen. Although some anecdotes may make it seem like we have all the answers, I assure you we do not. We still make mistakes—daily. But I hope our experiences will help you avoid common mistakes and try some approaches you hadn't considered before.

> I tended to compare my children to children in the public school more than to other homeschoolers when I first started. I was unsure of myself as a teacher. Were the methods I was using even going to teach him what he needed to know? Now, four years later, my son is learning how to write, knows how to read very well, and has learned quite a few more things. We didn't do it like the public school, yet he still learned! Starting to see the fruit of those first few years has really increased my confidence as a teacher.
> —Beth B., Minnesota

Also included are stories and insights from other "imperfect" homeschoolers. You'll find helpful suggestions and ideas, laugh at the stories of others, and mourn with those who have suffered—all while continuing to develop your own homeschooling philosophies.

The impossible goal of perfection can stress and harm families, but there are things you can do to be perfectly happy with your situation, make changes where possible, and discover a realistic vision of homeschooling for your family. This book is about creating a path of your own amid the maze of home education options and the challenges you'll encounter over the years. For the parents and children who will be influenced by this information, it is my prayer that you will be able to make a difference in the lives of generations to come.

Chapter 2

Pressure, Perfection, and Progress

While working on this book, I conducted a survey of homeschoolers across the United States. Among many things, I asked: "Do you think the standards placed on homeschoolers by society (friends, relatives, the educational community) are higher than those placed on other educators?" Of the hundreds who responded, 93 percent gave an affirmative response to this question. Sadly, these higher standards often add pressure on homeschooling families to prove they are doing a good job.

This is hardly encouraging news, but it is reality. And as this chapter will show, some pressures cannot be avoided. Still, I hope an honest look at common stressors in the life of homeschoolers will help you understand and deal realistically with challenges as they come up.

In my experience, quite a few people would

> I have not yet learned how to deal with the extra pressure of teaching, raising little people, and home-making all at once!
>
> —Linda G., South Africa

> Homeschoolers know that they are completely responsible for their child's education, which will affect their child's success as an adult. This is good, because with the realization of responsibility (pressure) comes a keen desire to make wise decisions regarding education and training.
>
> —Raleah M., Oklahoma

say the pressure on homeschooling families is warranted because those people generally think we do a poor job. The reality is that homeschoolers "typically score 15 to 30 percentile points above public-school students on standardized academic achievement tests," according to Brian Ray of the National Home Education Research Institute. Ray has also found that "homeschooled students score above average on achievement tests regardless of their parents' level of formal education or their family's household income."

Others might argue that society doesn't really place additional pressure on homeschooling families; it's simply a perception by homeschoolers that doesn't exist. However, the Home School Legal Defense Association regularly fields reports of social workers, truancy officers, legislators, school personnel, and others across the United States who are disregarding parental rights—particularly with regard to educational freedom. This is not perceived pressure. It is real. There have been cases of parents being wrongly charged with educational neglect, community centers refusing to allow homeschoolers to meet in their facilities, social workers pushing their way into private homes, and judges imposing fines on homeschool families. These are not isolated incidents. They occur in all fifty states throughout the year. Obviously, there are too many cases to list here, but anyone interested in reading about specific cases or legislation can visit the association's Web site at *www.hslda.org.*

Local school systems might also place unwarranted pressure on homeschooling families—for example, requesting information that is not required by law or reporting a homeschooled child for "truancy." There have also been instances of local education agencies imposing higher standards or additional requirements for homeschooled students wanting to enter public schools. In Washington County, Tennessee, in 2007 and 2008, homeschooled students trying to enter the local county public school mid-semester were told that since they had made a commitment to homeschooling, they could not enter public school until the next semester or the following year, thus denying the child their federally mandated right of access to public education.

PRESSURE

Beyond school systems and society in general, the pressure to excel at homeschooling, or even to defend your decision to home-school your children, can come from a variety of sources:

- Relatives
- Friends
- "Experts"
- Children
- Spouse
- Ourselves

It is a difficult situation if relatives don't support your decision to homeschool. They might try to not-so-subtly "test" your child's academic abilities ("Abby, how about reading this for me?") or question her socialization skills ("Tell me about your friends. ..."). They might take every opportunity to tell you stories about how homeschooling doesn't work, directly tell your child he or she should be in public school, or even threaten to report you to children's services.

Sometimes friends might be the ones who question your decision to homeschool. Over the years, I've discovered that the problem usually is not that they disagree with the concept of homeschooling, but they think *you* disapprove of *their* choice to send their child to public or private school. Each of you surely loves your child, and opinions differ on many parenting issues, including discipline, eating habits, and clothing choices. But strangely, while friends can politely disagree on many things, it's often education choices that cause relationship problems.

Expert Advice:
Encouraging or Discouraging?

Homeschoolers tell me about the pressure they sometimes feel from the homeschooling experts. Instead of feeling encouraged through various books, conferences, seminars, or other programs, many homeschoolers feel intimidated. A number of these experts travel from conference to conference with their polite children (who have perfected their math skills by helping sell products from the family business). It's difficult not to envy these families. Trust me, I know because I have! On the other hand, I've been on the other side of all of this. At times moms comment to me, "I would never be able to take care of the household, teach my children, cook, do all the other things I need to do, and write books like you do!" The fact is I can't do all these things either. When I'm finishing a big project like a book, other things have to wait—including a clean house and fresh-cooked meals.

God has given us all individual gifts. Some people are good at things like organization, public speaking, or writing, and have used these gifts to help other homeschooling families. But God has given homeschooling moms and dads many gifts to minister to others in needed ways: hospitality, cooking skills, musical talent, sports abilities; the list goes on and on. So rather than being intimidated by the experts, look in the mirror and recognize the many wonderful talents God has bestowed on that person looking back at you. Use your gifts to bless others.

If you're still feeling pressure because experts or others tell you to "do it this way" or "if you'd only follow my plan, your life will be perfect, your children will obey, and they will love learning" or any other "just do it my way" kinds of statements, my advice is simple: Find different experts!

Pressure to excel can also come from within your own home—from three unlikely sources: your children, your spouse, and yourself. They don't mean to, but children can add stress to the homeschooling environment by wanting outside lessons, expensive science equipment, access to extracurricular activities, and so on. The pressure to please your child can be strong, and sometimes his or her enthusiasm or desires exceeds a parent's stamina—or checking account.

An over-demanding spouse often leads to conflict in the home. Sometimes the husband pressures his wife to homeschool in a particular manner with specific results. He might question her abilities or criticize her daily achievements—or lack thereof. Other times, it's the wife who places undue pressure on her husband. She insists that he become more involved with their child's education, help select curriculum, and spend more time with the family. Some wives do this without taking into account their husband's other responsibilities and the stress he might feel, for example, as the primary breadwinner (in most cases).

Perhaps the biggest source of homeschooling pressure comes from within. We parents can be our own worst critics. When moms—or dads—place unreasonable expectations upon themselves, it creates a stressful environment. Too many families stop homeschooling simply because they don't think they are doing a "good enough" job.

So what can be done to counter all this undue pressure? With the various sources of stress affecting us in different ways, I have found it helpful to evaluate the issues individually and determine which ones are valid and need attention and which ones can be ignored.

I'm a list person, and when I'm stressed I make lists. If the house is dirty, I make a prioritized list of what to clean first. If the children are behind

> Homeschoolers are expected to be smarter and very well behaved.
>
> —Beth B., Minnesota

> Homeschooling is seen by so many people as a choice that is radical or even offensive. It sometimes seems as if they personally take offense when you say that you chose to homeschool your children. I think sometimes they feel that by your choosing differently from them, you are criticizing them personally.
>
> —Julie M., North Carolina

academically, I make a list of academic tasks they need to master. If I'm feeling pressure from people, I even list their comments or concerns and try to evaluate them honestly. Some comments I've heard are almost inconceivable, but others might mirror your own concerns, especially if you are considering homeschooling.

Comment / Concern	Valid concern or helpful comment?	Notes / Possible Action Response
"Your children will be 'backward' if you homeschool."	Yes	As you homeschool, expose your children to outside activities and fellowship opportunities.
"Your children won't know how to sit still in a classroom."	Yes	Train your children how to obey and sit still regardless of the environment.
"You don't feed the children enough."	No	A close relative said this because I wouldn't let the children eat snacks before dinner. The children eat plenty, just not junky snacks. This comment was very hurtful, but after evaluation, I decided there was no reason to change our healthy eating habits.
"The children are too polite."	No	We want our children to be polite and to say "Yes, ma'am" and "No, ma'am," even if someone else thinks it's old-fashioned.
"The children are rude."	No	The person who made this comment was stressed, and the children got on her nerves, but they were not being rude. Action: Help children know how to be extra polite when people don't feel well.
"What if the children fall behind academically?"	Yes	Watch children for signs that they are learning, even if your standards are different from someone else's. (We focus on character development more than academics in the early years.) Consider standardized tests each spring to evaluate their progress.

When evaluating comments that produce stress, be specific with the comment or concern and specific with your possible action or response. If something needs to be addressed, list several options for how to respond, talk with your spouse, pray about the issue (and the options), and then decide the best way to proceed.

Unfortunately, while we can evaluate the pressures that cause stress, we cannot always eliminate the source of the stress. As a homeschooling advocate, one of my greatest stressors relates to incorrect information being given to potential homeschooling parents. I can't stop this from happening, but all of us can work diligently toward making the public aware of the legality of home education, and we can provide resources so that potential homeschoolers can obtain accurate information. As a homeschooling mom, one of my greatest sources of stress relates to our family's irregular schedule. But with rotating work schedules, frequent illnesses, unannounced guests, and other challenges, it's almost impossible for us to maintain a regular schedule. We deal with it by being flexible.

> I think different expectations are placed on homeschoolers by different people. Homeschooling parents place quite high standards on themselves, whereas society and teachers expect that what homeschoolers must be doing has to be of a lower quality since they lack a teaching degree.
>
> —Tracey L., Australia, former primary-school teacher

PERFECTION

I think most of us homeschooling moms struggle with perfectionism. For some, it reveals itself in a perfectly clean home, possibly creating incredible stress if the home is not perfectly clean. For others, it surfaces as constant worry over what others think about their home-school household. For still others, perfectionism is manifested through strict schedules and rigorous academic training for the children.

A desire to attain perfection isn't necessarily bad. In some ways it is beneficial to push yourself to excel. And when it comes to homeschooling, perfectionistic parents might push their children to excel.

This isn't bad either, unless it is taken to the extreme. However, it's important to remember that while your child might make a perfect score on every spelling test, your house might be perfectly dust free, and you might have all your curriculum plans in perfect order, these times will likely be the exception rather than the rule—and that's okay.

Like many other homeschooling moms, Janice H. wanted everything perfect when she started homeschooling more than fifteen years ago. She remembers thinking her daughter would reach her full potential "if we played all the right games and put flash cards on the wall even before she could read [and] said our numbers in Spanish as we climbed up the stairs. . . ."

I've seen hundreds of moms do this over the years. Mom plans to start "school" with five-year-old Jacob in the fall, so she buys educational bulletin board materials, an ABC border for the wall, a little school desk, and then throws in some school supplies to round out the preparations. Now, there is nothing wrong with this. In fact, some families prefer to imitate a traditional school setting in their home, and others just want an atmosphere conducive to learning.

Still, after months of trying to create the perfect atmosphere, it wasn't how Janice wanted family life to be. "We see new homeschoolers and families in general starting off just like we did," Janice says. "The house must be perfect, the yard maintained immaculately, the family should be involved in every cultural enrichment program you can squeeze into the schedule, and they rarely have time to have dinner together. They put up a façade of perfection yet they are strangers living in the same home."

> When the kids were younger, I would sometimes have to hide out at lunchtime to pull myself together for the afternoon session.
>
> —Lisa A., Oklahoma

> When I get tired, or have too many other things to do, I don't handle the pressure well at all. I find myself getting angry with myself, kids, and hubby! I find myself saying things to the kids I shouldn't say. I lose my patience with them. I guess I put pressure on myself about things we must get done. But they don't really need to be done.
>
> —Pam B., New Zealand

Thankfully, more and more homeschooling families are following Janice's lead and giving up their dreams of perfection. Instead, they are focusing on their relationships with God, family, and others in the community. "So much knowledge is obtained by living our simple life," Janice says. "We avoid people that make us feel like we ought to be doing something better, faster, or more in-depth. We know better. That only leads to depression and an unnatural desire for things and ideas that we weren't meant for."

PROGRESS

Are you trying to overcome perfectionist tendencies? Do you really want a perfect homeschool household but realize it's not possible, so you want to learn how to be satisfied with life as it is? Do you want to learn ways to push your child yet not hold him up to unrealistic expectations with regard to academics, social issues, even life skills such as keeping his bedroom clean? The stress related to perfectionism comes from within. It's okay to reveal to others our true self—our imperfect home, imperfect children, imperfect home school, and imperfect marriage—and remove the mask of perfection.

As you consider your homeschool environment, think about your child's first accomplishments. You may recollect how as a baby your daughter gradually developed the ability to interact, sit up, and then crawl. You might recall how your newly adopted son began to make eye contact and then use words in English for the first time. You might remember the first time your daughter with special needs held her own fork at lunchtime. These accomplishments may

I think the main stress is a result of the pressure my wife feels about being the perfect teacher for our child and whether she is doing enough and how our child responds at times, i.e., not paying attention, getting distracted, and not following instructions. I handle this stress by making time to listen to my wife's concerns so she doesn't feel alone, volunteer my time to help so she gets a break, and discuss things with our child so that both mum and child can deal with the issues causing the stress.

—Iain S., New Zealand

have seemed insignificant to someone else, but you rejoiced because they were milestones for your child. I believe God sees our seemingly small accomplishments in the same way. The Bible says that only Christ was "without sin" (Hebrews 4:15). God doesn't expect us to be perfect.

You'll find ideas throughout this book to help you create your own path for your not-so-perfect homeschool household. Later chapters also include specific suggestions on dealing with stress related to academics, finances, health problems, and other challenges. Meanwhile, try to enjoy every moment with your family and focus on little steps of progress. I believe that as we rejoice in our children's achievements and turn our hearts, however slowly, toward our heavenly Father, he rejoices with us.

My biggest stress was probably feeling inadequate at times. While I now see that I've gone beyond my wildest expectations, I would constantly feel as if I didn't know as much as my friends who attended public school.

—Mandee W., age 20, former homeschool student

We have very little stress with regard to the schooling itself. The only issue that keeps cropping up is [my wife's] self doubts. She has such a strong desire to educate our children so that they reach their highest potential, she sometimes wonders if she is failing them, and her doubts can get her down.

—Bryan D., Tennessee

Chapter 3

Developing Positive Relationships

Several years ago a mom came to me and asked how she should start homeschooling her children, then ages six and four. I suggested three things: reading to them frequently, training them to obey, and spending the first year or two focusing on relationships. In my opinion, it is that third step that isn't emphasized enough in homeschool households. We forget how important it is to teach our children how to get along, respect one another, and love others. Parents have plenty of time to introduce academics, field trips, and outside activities, but if children don't learn how to develop positive relationships while they are young, it is difficult for them to attain this ability later.

I ran into the same mom some years later. She had followed my advice and thanked me for helping her children become great friends. She read to them a lot and taught them to obey, but in teaching them to respect and care for one another and others, including the Lord, she gave a gift they will carry into adulthood and every relationship.

As wonderful as this may sound, I'm sure things weren't always smooth in this family's household. Every home has its share of conflicts. The question is how do we win—or better yet, avoid—the battles?

COUCH TIME

When our two oldest children were little, they had spats like all children do. If one child pushed another child, for example, or hurt his or her feelings in some way, they would get "couch time"—meaning they would have to sit on the couch and hold hands until they worked out their differences. Sometimes it took thirty seconds, and they would be giggling and laughing as if nothing ever happened. Sometimes they would sit for ten or fifteen minutes until they were ready to apologize. No matter how long it took, they were forced to resolve their differences if they wanted to get off the couch. Although couch time is not foolproof (you'll still have disagreements), I believe it has helped our children develop positive relationships with each other because we didn't allow wounds to fester.

PRACTICE APOLOGIES

It's a debate that never ends: Should we force children to apologize to each other or not? Some parents say no, because the child might not truly be sorry, and we're encouraging her to lie. Others say children need to practice apologies so they will get into the habit of apologizing.

For many parents, the key to this issue is that we never truly know what is in a child's heart. Whether he apologizes and means it is something that has to be between him and the Lord. In our family, we make our children apologize. However, we are careful about two things that usually indicate where a child's heart is: the wording of his apology and tone of his voice. If a child is being sassy or rude during an apology, a private discussion with the child about repentance is beneficial before having him apologize again.

Have you heard your child say something like this: "I'm sorry you were in my way and I hit you" or "I'm sorry you made me mad"? That's why the wording of apologies matters. Excusing your own behavior in an apology is obviously not an apology. For this reason, we remind the children that a true apology focuses on what they did, and then the other person will also be accountable for his or her own actions. Each person must ask forgiveness for his own transgressions. If a child is innocent, then his responsibility is simply forgiveness of the transgression.

SERVE ONE ANOTHER

When people join the Peace Corps or go on mission trips, they frequently develop strong bonds with the people they serve. Jesus was a great leader, but he was also very quick to serve! This same principle can be used to develop a positive relationship between siblings. When people serve one another, they develop a deeper relationship through action (being the server) and gratitude (being served).

Here are some ways to encourage children to serve one another:

- Have children take turns attending to needs at the dinner table.
- Assign an older child as a "buddy" to a younger child.
- Ask an older child to read aloud to a younger sibling.
- Have children practice flash cards, multiplication tables, or recitations together.
- Encourage your child to send notes or give gifts to another child.

REMIND THEM OF THEIR RELATIONSHIPS

Positive sibling relationships are so important in the short term and long term that when we did foster care, one of the first things we learned was that siblings are placed together (unless extreme circumstances require their separation, such as one child abusing another). Through words and actions, do your best to encourage good relationships between your kids, even reminding them of their special bond:

Biological siblings share DNA, making them more likely to look alike, have similar academic abilities, and have a tendency toward similar health issues. (This would make a great science or health lesson, by the way!)

Whether biological or adoptive, siblings share their parents. As their parents grow older, siblings may be called on to make decisions about how to care for their aging parents.

Siblings share a common history. While others see your family life from the outside, siblings are the only ones who actually share the experience with you. We remind our children that one day, when we are gone, they will be the only people who will truly know what it was like to grow up as a Haskins kid. They will be able to share stories with others who were not a part of that history or only experienced it on the outskirts.

Siblings have a responsibility to one another. We teach our kids that if they see someone picking on their brother or sister, it is their responsibility to try to stop the harassment. We also try to make them understand that aggravating or insulting their own brothers or sisters is not

> I have the opportunity to be with my children every day and night except for the sixteen hours a week that I work outside my home. I feel that I am more in-tune to my children's needs, strengths, and weaknesses. For example, I can tell when they have individually had enough. I can see it in their actions, sounds, faces. So yes, I do feel that I relate to them better because I have to learn to live with them. Except for work, I don't get a break. I have to know when someone has reached their boiling point (including myself) and I have to act quickly. But I am a parent, and just like other parents, I do make mistakes. You just learn from it and go on.
>
> —Julie M., North Carolina

acceptable. If the relationship between siblings isn't mended, a permanent rift can result. You have probably seen this in families where adult siblings still can't get along because of teasing or harassment that occurred twenty or thirty years earlier. When siblings stand up for each other, they learn to trust one another, laying the foundation for a positive relationship as the years go by.

AVOID COMPARISONS

An important way to help your children and their relationships is to avoid comparing one child to another. When a parent voices negative comparisons—or even positive ones—the child may think he is not accepted for the individual he is. Every child is unique and a blessing from the Creator. The Bible says, "For you created my inmost being; you knit me together in my mother's womb" (Psalm 139:13). In a family with more than one child, where children already share space in their home, their toys, their parents, and almost everything else that comes along, brothers and sisters can and will assert their individuality.

Parents who compare a child's negative behavior to another child's positive behavior run the risk of creating animosity between the children. The child with negative behavior certainly is going to develop a sense of resentment toward the "good" sibling, and she is going to think her parents do not love and accept her for who she is. The child with positive behavior could also be harmed, as she may develop a sense of pride or haughtiness. Even comparisons made regarding positive behavior can create a sense that the child isn't loved and appreciated for his uniqueness but rather for how he can perform, look, or behave like another sibling, especially if that sibling is older.

Starting with our first child, Sarah, my husband and I made a commitment to avoid comparisons in our family. We make a point of telling each child that we love him or her and greatly appreciate their uniqueness. We also try our best to encourage each child in his or her individual interests and talents. We've had much less success convincing our relatives to avoid comparing our children—to each other, to us, even to distant relatives whom we've never met. Some comparisons could be harmless ("She plays well alone, just like I used to do when I was her age"), while others border on the ridiculous ("He has your great-great-granddaddy's feet!"). Still, when conversations go in this direction, we quickly find some way to politely excuse ourselves so that we don't have to endure an analysis of every character trait our children exhibit, every body part they possess, and every talent they've ever demonstrated.

EQUAL VS. FAIR TREATMENT

If you think about it, the popular advice to treat children equally is impossible. Even trying to treat children equally—or worse, telling children they are going to get equal treatment—sets families up for failure, particularly in the area of sibling relationships.

Yes, we parents should treat our children fairly, but there is a huge difference between fair and equal. Fairness ensures that all children will be loved, nurtured, and encouraged, even if a toddler receives a kiss on the cheek and a teen receives a pat on the shoulder. They will be disciplined when they misbehave, even if one child is put in the corner and the other is made to sit on the couch. When they get material gifts, it may mean one child receives a drum set and the other receives art lessons. Equality implies that if one child gets a book at the used bookstore, the other one will get one as well. As you perhaps well know, the problem with equality is that children are clever enough to figure out that we can't make everything truly equal. They will look for any discrepancy in our actions. One child's book might have a torn page or scribbling in it. If the books have different titles, one child might decide on the way home that he likes the other child's book better.

Equality really becomes a problem in situations where one child is invited to a birthday party, has an opportunity to attend camp, or wins an ice-cream party with her friends at Vacation Bible School. Should parents find a way to make sure each child in the family can participate in the same activities or do something similar? Of course not. In our family we gently remind the other children that they will have an opportunity to do something fun in the future and encourage them to be happy for their brother or sister. Encouraging children to be content with what they have and happy when others are blessed helps develop a sense of peace in their lives, regardless of the circumstances.

In a homeschool setting, fair versus equal treatment is also important because children's personalities and interests are different. One child might want to be in every sport and activity possible, and though you may want to encourage this, what do you do with the child who has no desire to do these things? As we discussed, God has given each of us unique gifts. So while you spend money on athletic fees for one child, it's okay to buy books and science equipment for another child.

Finally, sibling rivalry can be reduced if we help children understand that they are ready for different things at different times. For example, one child may be responsible enough to take on a part-time job when she turns fourteen, while her sister wasn't ready until she was sixteen. Another example: It is fair to allow one child to have a pet if she has shown that she can be responsible for its care, while forbidding the other children pets until they are old enough and able to care for them responsibly.

PROMOTE TEAMWORK

Healthy competition can be fun, but if sibling rivalry is an issue in your home, focus on activities and games that promote teamwork rather than competition. Play games that develop trust and require working together, such as three-legged races, relay races, treasure hunts in groups, scavenger hunts in pairs, tag games that require one child to "unfreeze" another, and educational team games such as Cranium. Not only do these activities promote bonding, but they can count as instructional time through physical education, social skills, and math skills (lots of board games incorporate math skills).

Additionally, while we generally do not encourage electronic entertainment, our children always seem to bond when it comes to the television or computer. Our boys usually enjoy lots of argument-free fun times when they play computer games together. They are not competing against one another, but they work together to defeat a common enemy: the computer. We also let them pick movies to watch together. If they argue over the choice, though, they don't get to watch it (discipline that "fits the crime").

Teamwork can also be promoted through other homeschool activities; for example, math speed drills. The child completes the same speed drill each day for a week and you keep track of the number of problems she completes correctly in a set time period (usually five minutes). Children enjoy seeing their individual scores improve from day to day, but you can also keep track of group scores. If you have more than one child, add the scores together, and for each day that they improve their group score, offer some sort of reward (a treat, playtime, extra computer time). When you start with new speed drills the next week, begin with fresh scores. (We keep track of scores for each month on a large dry-erase calendar.)

For families with one or two children, encourage these same activities when other children are in your home. Also, take advantage of play dates, co-op settings, and other group opportunities to ensure that your child develops her teamwork skills. (More on co-ops and other homeschool activities outside the home is found in chapter 6.)

THE PARENT-CHILD RELATIONSHIP

When parents start teaching their child at home, one of the first things they realize is how it affects the parent-child relationship in unique ways. Homeschooling can produce incredible bonds within the family, but the frequent contact can also bring stress to the parent *and* the child.

One shock for new homeschooling parents is how busy they are and how much time they must invest in their children. This is true whether you have one child or ten, a structured curriculum, or no set structure at all. Parenting is a lot of work. Homeschooling is parenting to the extreme!

For some moms, motherhood itself is stressful. If this describes you, please know it doesn't mean you aren't meant for homeschooling. Nor does it mean you don't love your child or children. It may simply mean you would occasionally like to go to the bathroom alone without little fingers poking under the door. There are some suggestions later in this chapter on how to deal with the stresses of being together day in and day out.

Many moms who transition directly to homeschooling after the preschool/kindergarten years are excited to "officially" start homeschooling. They invest all their time and energy into selecting curriculum, designing unit studies, taking the child on educational field trips, and preparing a learning area. These are wonderful activities, and I encourage parents to enjoy these preparations. Difficulties can arise, however, when Mom invests so much time in these activities that she neglects other responsibilities, such as the relationship with her husband. She can also become so involved in preparing her child's "school" that she replaces a nurturing environment with so much structure that the child begins to feel resentful.

After a few months of homeschooling, these same moms often experience burnout because the five-year-old who was so happy and excited about learning in August suddenly is sullen and withdrawn by March. It's at this stage that many families decide they weren't meant to homeschool. But maybe they were! These families have simply forgotten to focus on relationships first, academics second.

RELATIONSHIPS AS YOU TRANSITION TO HOMESCHOOLING

Family dynamics can really change when you start homeschooling, especially if your child has been attending public or private school for nearly eight hours a day. In a way, both parent and child have to adjust to each other, and for some moms, it is difficult to sacrifice alone time for child time. Other common adjustments include having a messier home, needing to spend money on books and educational supplies, and having children study things Mom or Dad know little about. On top of all this, the whole family has to adjust to Mom (or Dad) as the primary teacher. While many "experts" advocate setting up a separate schoolroom, calling the husband the "principal," and making the children refer to Mom as "teacher," all this does is create a traditional school setting in the home environment. It might be more beneficial in the long term to use some of the following suggestions:

- Take some time off. When children come out of a traditional school environment, it often helps for them to have some downtime before starting homeschool lessons. Some people call this de-schooling.

- Tell your child the plan. Any child old enough to have been in a traditional school setting is old enough to understand what homeschooling is. For younger students, you might simply choose to tell them that you're going to have lots of fun at home and they don't have to ride the bus anymore or miss Mom all day. For older students, you may need to explain a plan that will allow them to continue social activities with their friends through co-op classes, sports, church, and other outlets.

- Consider letting your student help decide which subjects he will study. This is a great way to get a child excited about homeschooling quickly. Rather than studying "science," he can experiment with robotics. Rather than studying "history," he can study about the Renaissance. You get the idea.

PARENT AS TEACHER

When you homeschool, you have a unique relationship with your child that involves all the responsibilities of parenting (discipline, advice, nurturing), in addition to the responsibilities of educating your child. As mentioned, homeschooling changes family dynamics, but the long-term benefits to the parent-child relationship far outweigh any difficulties you'll face.

Perhaps you sense this already, but just because you have officially started homeschooling (whether or not your child has ever been in another school setting), it doesn't mean that now you have to go from being the nurturing, loving mom your child has always known to some sort of educational dictator. Let your child know you will always and forever be his or her mom or dad first. Show your child that you love him—even if he does write the letter *j* backward or has trouble reciting yesterday's Bible verse. Encourage your child. Be there for your child. Train your child. But always remember that our heavenly Father loved us enough to sacrifice his own Son so that we could know him better. Focus on relationships first, academics second.

My relationship with my boys (who are home-schooled) and with my two younger children (institutional schooling) is most definitely different. WhIle I can't graph it, I can feel it. The depth of our knowledge of each other has increased. I can't hide who I am from children who are with me all day. They can't hide who they are. I see their strengths and their weaknesses, and they see mine. This transparency leads to the understanding that love is unconditional, for better or for worse, within our family. While the world and institutions set conditions on acceptance, the home does not. Rules are rules and love is love.

—Tamiko C., British Columbia

Many parents are eager to have their children start learning academics; some think the younger the better. However, if a child doesn't develop strong relationships during his or her early years, emotional, developmental, and behavioral problems are likely to crop up for the rest of his or her life. God created the family, and he placed parents in the unique position to develop this bond with their children. Nurture the relationship with your child first and then watch his cues for the appropriate time to teach him how to read, begin violin lessons, or learn double-digit addition.

RELATIONSHIP-INDUCED STRESS

When families spend time together day in and day out, there is a tendency to develop relationship-induced stress. Here are some ideas to help deal with relational stresses:

- Establish an "alone" place in the house. This could be a bathroom, bedroom, laundry room, or any place that provides a few minutes of privacy for the parent.

- If family members need a break from one another, send the children to sit on their beds for a while and read a book, color, or play quietly with a toy.

- Allow members of the household to request personal space. If this means someone needs ten minutes alone, try to respect this request.

- Encourage grandparents or other trusted adults to develop strong bonds with your child. Relationships like these can allow the homeschooling parent to take breaks and provide trustworthy mentors for your child.

- If Mom does most of the teaching and is having difficulty with the child, encourage Dad to spend time alone with the child (or vice versa if Dad is the main teacher). Just make sure you don't allow the child to start manipulating you into triangular discussions.

DAD TIME

While many dads are amazingly active in homeschool family life, moms usually shoulder most of the responsibility of teaching, particularly when the children are younger. This doesn't mean dads can't be involved with the children's education. On the contrary, a dad can help in many ways! His assistance is a stress relief for Mom and helps him get to know his children better, encourages a positive relationship between family members, and maintains his connection to homeschool activities. Here are a few ways dads can be involved:

- Coach the child's sport team.
- Help the child with a subject in which Dad has expertise.
- Be the designated assistant for science fair projects, art projects, etc.
- Read bedtime stories to the children each night.
- Lead family devotions.
- Take child for walks when Mom needs a break.
- Intervene if children are bickering.
- Intervene if child is being disrespectful to Mom.
- Discipline a child when necessary.
- Take Mom out for time alone (date night or other activity).
- Volunteer to teach a class at co-op.
- Volunteer to teach a class at your home with other homeschoolers present.
- Teach a subject to the children based on Dad's interests (computers, science, nature, writing).

As children grow older, their interests sometimes fall in line with one parent or another, or their knowledge in certain subjects surpasses the primary teacher. When our eleven-year-old son begins to talk about a subject out of my range of expertise, I send him to his father. When he throws out words like *transformer, fuel cells,* and *electric generator motor,* I have no idea what he is talking about! When Chris isn't around, I listen to my son intently and just nod my head in amazement. I'm thankful my husband understands at least some of what the child is talking about, and one of my husband's jobs is to handle all the electronic, automobile, airplane, fuel, scientific, and computer discussions.

In many families, when children reach junior high or high school age, the other parent (often the dad) takes over much of the teaching. This is a terrific option for some families, and even when Mom is still the main teacher, it's great to rely on Dad to answer questions, lead family discussions about certain topics, or be a part of new activities. Now that our daughter is in high school, she goes to Civil Air Patrol meetings once a week with my husband. The thirty-minute drive is a great opportunity for Chris and Sarah to talk, and it also gives him a chance to be out of the house one evening each week.

As mentioned earlier, it's not unusual to experience homeschool burnout or get just plain frustrated with all the responsibilities. Moms remember life before homeschooling, and it's natural to sometimes feel like you just need some space. Even an occasional five or ten minutes to regain your composure is enough to help you maintain your sanity, but sometimes more is necessary. If that's the case, consider joining some sort of group for moms (a quilting bee, for example), take a class at your local community college, or schedule a weekend away with a friend or some other homeschooling moms. If these activities aren't an option, you might even consider finding a chat room on the Internet

> Enjoy each other. Homeschooling is a wonderful opportunity to build relationships and foster love and peace among family members. Provide much encouragement and physical love; generously dole out hugs and kisses with words of praise. Number one on my priority list of things to do together is READ. Snuggle up and share great books, beginning with the Bible.
>
> —Susie D., Tennessee

with like-minded moms who can empathize with your situation. I almost hesitate to mention that because I'm not a fan of chat rooms, but I realize for some moms who live in rural areas or who are not yet connected with other homeschooling families, this might be a positive option.

Chapter 4

The Socialization Question

When I meet people and they discover that we homeschool, the first question is almost always, "But what about socialization?" Some are simply curious, but typically the question reflects the myth that home-schooled children are awkward, different, or unsocialized. So if the question comes up, or you are new to homeschooling and wondering about it yourself, here are some ideas as to why homeschoolers are actually better socialized than children in institutional school settings.

- Homeschooled children are usually exposed to a greater variety of social settings, such as trips to the store, the bank, the library, rather than sitting in a classroom all day.

- The average homeschooler comes in contact with people of different age groups more frequently than other children.

- Homeschoolers typically take more field trips and are much more involved in community activities than other children.

- Homeschoolers are more often active in and aware of government and social issues than other children.

- The average young person who attends institutional school settings spends almost eight hours each day with their same-age peers for an average of one hundred eighty days of the year for twelve or more years of their life. They are able to associate with same-age peers, but they often do not have much opportunity to interact with people outside their peer group. Homeschoolers typically have very close relationships with their parents and other adults.

- Homeschoolers are usually around younger children more frequently, which better prepares them for when they have their own families. Children in public schools may receive classes on parenting. Homeschool students receive regular hands-on preparation in child care, parenting, and home-making skills.

- On average, the homeschool sibling relationship is closer than that of other children because they spend so much more time with their siblings. True friendships with home-school siblings are common.

- Homeschoolers are usually taught to question and research what they learn and not simply accept something for fact without proof to back up theories. This questioning nature enables them to discuss ideas with other people.

In fact, research by the National Home Education Research Institute indicates that homeschooling prepares children for the responsibilities of adult life. Adults who were taught at home typically:

- participate in local community service more frequently than does the general population;

- vote and attend public meetings more frequently than the general population;

- go to and succeed in college at an equal or higher rate than the general population;

- internalize the values and beliefs of their parents at a very high rate.

Unfortunately, some people have encountered homeschoolers whom they deem "weird" or "different." They interpret this as a sign that the student lacks socialization skills. In response, I like to point out that being different isn't necessarily a bad thing! If you are a Christian homeschooling family, there should be a difference in your behavior as compared to those around you! Personally, I am proud that my children's behavior is noticeably different from others' (at least most of the time).

One day I had a discussion with a public schoolteacher that put this issue in perspective. Like many teachers I've met, this man, who taught at the junior high level, opposed home education. When I asked him why, he said the homeschoolers who came into his classroom lacked socialization skills. They were very smart, obedient, and well-behaved in the classroom, but they didn't know how to "associate" with their peers. He shared an example of a homeschooled girl who had returned to public school at the beginning of the year. On the playground during recess, the girl would typically stand off by herself or talk with the teachers.

When I asked what the other students were doing, he said the girls and boys would break off into separate groups, as is typical in sixth grade, and chat. He told me the girls talked about things like boyfriends, cell phones, dating, makeup, and clothes. The teacher described all his concerns, and then I offered him this perspective:

> In public schools... a child spends the day being told not to talk, not to interact, not to socialize. Socialization is allowed to occur during lunchtime and recess time, but on a limited and controlled basis. Socialization, when it occurs, is with children of the same age and from the same neighborhood. With a minimum amount of effort, a homeschooled child can be involved in activities with children from different backgrounds and of different ages.
>
> —Jennifer S., Maryland, former teacher in public and private school settings, now a homeschooling mom

Did you ever stop to think that perhaps the girl is actually too mature for these students? Think about this for a minute: I have a twelve-year-old daughter, and we have tried to train her to stay away from questionable behavior or discussions. As a matter of fact, we tell our children to flee from sin. If she were in a group of girls and they began talking about boys, makeup, or those other things you mentioned, I would honestly hope that she could find better things to do. We've taught our daughter that courtship (getting to know a young man through supervised activities and with parental permission) is acceptable, but dating (time spent alone with someone of the opposite sex for the purpose of developing a relationship) is not; cell phones are acceptable for adults, but not children; beauty is something that comes from within, not something that is attained through makeup or brand-name clothing. You see, the real problem isn't that these children aren't socialized. The real problem is that the children share different values and fundamental beliefs about what's appropriate. Perhaps these homeschoolers you're so concerned about simply have a different set of morals, and they have chosen not to "socialize" with other kids who do not share or who oppose their values.

Of course, social skills do not come naturally to every child—homeschooled or not. There are times when homeschooling parents should be genuinely concerned about their child's socialization skills. Jennifer M., of Columbia, Maryland, grew up being homeschooled, but this fact didn't make the decision to teach her own children at home any easier.

"I was very concerned about socialization," she says. "I was severely lacking in social skills when I started college."

She and her husband eventually decided to homeschool, and they have addressed Jennifer's concerns about socialization by enrolling their son in many outside activities, including physical education, art and music lessons, foreign language classes, and science labs.

Whether your child is just starting kindergarten or entering junior high, the following sections include ideas to help develop his or her social skills. Interacting with others is important, but children tend to imitate those around them, so any child can learn to communicate appropriately based on his or her parents' example.

SIGNS OF HEALTHY SOCIAL SKILLS

Social skills make it possible for a person to interact and communicate with others in an appropriate manner. The following list has been slightly adapted from various lists of social skill goals. Students should be able to:

- take turns
- share with others
- use appropriate language
- use appropriate voice tone (yelling outside, quiet talk inside)
- say "please" and "thank you"
- praise others and avoid insults
- ask for help when needed
- stay on task
- look at others when spoken to
- communicate clearly
- wait patiently for lunch
- take care of belongings
- listen attentively
- resolve conflicts appropriately (no hitting, no biting)
- follow directions

- work with a team
- share ideas coherently
- understand age-appropriate social concepts
- help others

Every social skill on this list can be achieved as you homeschool your child. You may want to find opportunities for your child to play with other children. You will most likely want to introduce your child to various social environments. And you will surely want to practice proper social skills in the home, but however you introduce social skills to your child, homeschooling is one of the best ways to ensure that your child develops the skills he or she needs to do well in life.

Friends and Acquaintances

The social opportunities that children receive in public school settings are planned out: recess time, snack time, lunchtime, etc. For the homeschooled child, you can also plan social opportunities. Here are some suggestions:

- Join a homeschool support group so your child will have playmates.
- Join a co-op where your child can take classes. (In a co-op, homeschool parents come together to teach classes cooperatively to their group of children.)
- Organize play dates with friends.
- If there is a fine arts center in your area, enroll your child in art or music lessons.
- Sign your child up for karate, gymnastics, or horseback riding lessons.
- Let your child play a sport.

- If you live in a neighborhood, make an effort to meet other children in the neighborhood.

- Visit local parks and introduce yourself and your child to other moms and their children.

- Find out if there is a drop-off play center in your area and take your child there on occasion.

- Encourage your child to participate in a youth group.

- Encourage older children to take on a part-time job where other young people work.

- Volunteer for the summer at a local historic site that has other young volunteers.

- Audition to be in a local or regional play or musical concert with others the same age.

- For older students, call the local middle or high school and find out about extracurricular activities (4-H, Civil Air Patrol, volunteering at a hospital) available to students in the area that are not affiliated with the school system.

- If you live in a rural area, find a pen pal for your child. (Monitor correspondence if you don't know the family.)

One thing we do to ensure that our children are able to cultivate friendships and spend time with other children besides their siblings is by offering to baby-sit our friends' children. It gives the children an opportunity to play, and we enjoy having guests, so we do this on a regular basis. It also blesses the other family, since the mom and dad can go on a date, take an out-of-town trip, or spend time at home alone for a while. A good friend of mine told me several years ago that not everyone enjoys watching other people's children like we do, so this might not be your cup of tea, and that's okay too! Perhaps you can find a friend who likes having children

One benefit in home education is the lack of peer influence. Our older children, however, shared that they were too sheltered, so much so that they did not relate to peers in college. The challenge of fostering friendships outside the home that would encourage and not undermine our values was stressful.

—Gordon M., Tennessee

This is our ninth year homeschooling. Looking from the outside in, we look like we have it totally together. In reality we are often a total gong show. When your peers seem to be homeschooling so much better than you, it's important to remember that odds are high it's only the illusion you are getting while looking over another's fence.

—Deb B., Canada

visit, and let them go to their house. That way your child still gets to play with someone.

If you are new to an area and don't know many families, it might be difficult to find friends for your child at first. When Sarah was small, I remember being decidedly frustrated that we had no friends! Chris and I married a year after college. We lived with an elderly woman for about seven months, and then found out that I was pregnant. By the time Sarah was born and I had quit work, we had moved three times, no longer had contact with work friends, and hadn't met any new friends. For the next several years we tried to make friends. I joined a MOPS (Mothers of Preschoolers) group that met a few times each month. We also participated in church activities. I put Sarah in gymnastics lessons for a time. Before long, we had two more children. I still didn't have any real friends for myself or the children (though I'm sure our youngest two didn't mind). Finally I joined a homeschool group and became an active participant for the next eight years. That was a good outlet for us. For you, the answer might be in sports, clubs, art, or music, or some other area where you and your child have an opportunity to meet and interact with others.

Field Trips

We'll discuss field trips in more detail in chapters 6 and 7, but with regard to socialization, field trips are one of the best ways to introduce your child to society. Many people wrongly think of socialization as the ability to get along with one's peers. While this is a key aspect of socialization, it is just as important for a child to know how to respond in situations that involve people of various ages and backgrounds. When you take field trips with your child, you are exposing him to society. That will promote the development of social skills.

Practicing Social Skills

If you're concerned that your child lacks certain skills, make a concentrated effort to focus on those particular social skills in your home.

In younger grades in public school settings, teachers encourage role playing as the children pretend to be firefighters, nurses, construction workers, and even mommies and daddies. They make pretend phone calls, buy food at pretend stores, put baby dolls in cribs, and "cook" with child-sized appliances. This allows children to encounter different situations and put themselves "in the shoes," so to speak, of the other person so that they can better understand the roles of various members of society. Taking turns allows the children to practice different roles. These activities are part of socialization, and many skills can be learned through role playing and repeated practice.

Here are some ideas that you can do at home:

- Collect an assortment of dress-up clothes.

- Encourage your child's pretend play.

- Keep sheets and blankets handy to build forts.

- Let your child plan lunch (even if it means making peanut butter sandwiches).

- Practice phone skills through role playing and then let your child practice answering real calls while you supervise.

- Allow your child to push the buttons on the debit machine at the store.

- For older children, encourage them to create a newspaper for your home (small scale) or community (large scale) and report the latest news, events, etc.

- Make a lemonade stand in summer. This is great for role playing business skills, practicing mathematics, and interacting with people.

- Provide toys that encourage pretend play, such as dolls, Playmobil, Fisher-Price toys (castles, dollhouses, ships, etc.), and child-sized furniture.

Role playing can take many forms, depending on the age of the child. For younger children, they can be transported to an imaginary world with a fort, a few dress-up clothes, or even a stick that functions as a pretend sword. Children may continue to enjoy role playing or pretend play even into their early teens. When older children stay home alone, practice driving for the first time, or obtain their first baby-sitting job, this is also a form of role playing. They are practicing skills that they will need as adults. These are all beneficial activities.

COMMON QUESTIONS AND POSSIBLE RESPONSES

If you've been teaching at home for a while, you've likely heard a plethora of questions about homeschooling from friends and others. Some questions, especially personal ones from strangers, can put you on the defensive. The following are suggestions that might help you formulate appropriate responses of your own.

Q. Why aren't you in school (directed toward the children)?

A. A school is simply a place where some children learn. Since we homeschool, the world is our classroom and we consider everything a learning opportunity.

Q. What makes homeschoolers think they can teach their children better than trained professionals?

A. There are several reasons, but basically it boils down to this: Since parents love their child more than anyone else, they are naturally inclined to do everything in their power to see that the child receives the best education possible in a manner that meets the needs of that individual child in a nurturing environment.

> I would never ask people about why they would send their kids to [public] school, so why do people feel they can put down homeschooling and [question] what we do?
>
> —Pam B., New Zealand

Q. How do you teach subjects about which you know nothing or very little?

A. Sometimes homeschooled children surpass their parents in knowledge of a subject, but students can then study material on their own, as many of the great men and women in history have done. Additionally, homeschooling parents can and do take advantage of outside classes, tutors, video courses, online courses, and even dual enrollment college courses to teach students material that they might be uncomfortable teaching or lack the knowledge to teach. (State laws vary regarding the use and reporting of various supplemental educational options, so parents should confirm that these types of courses will be accepted as part of your child's educational portfolio.)

Q. Are all those children really yours (typically asked of parents with more than four children)?

A. You could say that you've stolen a few or that your friends loaned you some extra children to make your trip to the store more interesting. You could look around blankly and ask, "What children?" But probably the best way to respond is: Yes, they are indeed all our children, and we are very thankful that the Lord has blessed us with each and every one of them.

Q. I'm glad they're yours and not mine. I can barely handle two children. (This isn't a question, but it is a common comment.)

A. Many parents choose to respond sarcastically to comments of this nature, but that simply slams a door in the face of the other parent. It might be better to say something like: Yes, there have been times when I've questioned my ability as a parent, but parenting a large family can be such a joy (and then share examples of those joys).

Q. I thought all homeschoolers had big families. Why do you only have two children?

A. Just like other families, homeschooling families come in all shapes and sizes. You certainly don't have to have a lot of children in order to homeschool.

Q. With one child, isn't he (or she) lonely all day without siblings or other classmates to play with?

A. Actually, there are many advantages to homeschooling an only child. He gets lots of individualized attention during his lessons. He still has plenty of access to other people through his outside lessons and activities, including Boy Scouts, church, and baseball, so there are numerous social opportunities. He also plays with neighborhood friends after they come home from school.

Q. Why do you all dress the same? Don't you allow your children to show any individuality?

A. When I look at my family, I see a lot of individuality. Each child has his or her own personality, preferences, talents, etc. Sometimes they enjoy dressing alike or doing the same activities. Sometimes they don't. Actually, I think this is an odd question considering the fact that the typical teen crowd consists of kids wearing similar clothing, carrying the same type of bags, and playing with the same electronic gadgets.

Chapter 5

Routines and Schedules

Some homeschoolers live by schedules and love them! Others treat them like an assault upon their freedom. Since my goal is to help you find your own way, I'm not going to tell you whether to use a schedule or not, or if you do choose to follow a daily schedule, which one you should use. However, homeschooling families' schedules are among the most requested resources from new and veteran homeschoolers, so I am going to provide sample schedules. Even if you have no intention of using a schedule, hopefully you'll still find some helpful ideas. (If the thought of schedules starts to make your head hurt, just skip to the next chapter.)

YEARLY ROUTINES

While some states have requirements about the daily or yearly homeschool schedule, others do not. The main yearly routines that people use are:

- Four-day schedule with year-round schooling

- Five-day schedule with traditional 36-week, 180-day attendance, and summer break
- Year-round schedule with a week-long break every three weeks
- Year-round schedule with breaks as needed
- One month of school, two-week break, one month of school, two-week break, throughout the year.

Please recognize that while many homeschoolers follow these schedules with zeal, others take a more relaxed view of homeschooling. Unless your state specifies otherwise, you might decide to integrate worksheets, workbooks, and curriculum into your homeschooling when you believe your child needs some extra practice while using field trips, good books, and hands-on activities for your regular homeschool activities. You could do this and follow one of the above routines, or you might consider every day an opportunity to teach your child.

Learn to say no. This is your family's time. Others seem to think that since we're home all day we can baby-sit their children all the time or we can go to every women's Bible study.... Non-homeschooling families seem to think that just because we're home we have all the free time in the world to do other things. What they fail to remember is that, yes, we're home, but we're HOMESCHOOLING! We're not sitting around watching soap operas and waiting for the phone to ring.

—Kim W., Ohio

For some families, like ours, a flexible yearly routine with a relaxed approach to homeschooling works best. A flexible yearly routine works particularly well for families who travel a lot, who deal with a lot of health issues, or where the mom or dad has a seasonal job.

TIME SPENT ON EACH SUBJECT

The amount of time that homeschoolers spend on each subject is going to vary. In some states, the law actually specifies which subjects you have to study, and in some cases they tell you how much time you have to spend studying each day. However, one thing I like to remind new homeschooling parents is that "schooltime" can include many things, not just academics. Consider the things that count toward required hours for students in traditional school settings: videos, recess, lunch, study hall, lectures, transition time between classes, pep rallies, etc. In some states, the law specifies that daily "instructional time" must be four hours. Even with this specification, however, it's important to know what is instructional. I talk more about this in chapter 7.

Since a number of parents have asked for a list of how much time other homeschoolers spend on each subject, here is a general guide:

- Preschool: spend lots of time reading aloud to your child
- Kindergarten: 5 to 10 minutes per subject with frequent breaks
- Grades 1–3: 10 to 20 minutes per subject with frequent breaks
- Grades 4–5: 20 to 30 minutes per subject with regular breaks
- Grades 6–8: 30 to 45 minutes per subject with breaks as needed
- High school: 45 minutes or more as needed per subject to complete assignments

Bear in mind that you do not need to cover every subject every day and you don't need to do schoolwork every day. This is just a general guide based on the average abilities of children in each grade level. You will want to adjust the time you spend with each student on each subject based on his or her learning style, concentration abilities, fine and gross motor skills, and so on.

One thing frequently overlooked is that just because you want your first grader to do ten minutes of math per day, it doesn't mean that little Jacob has to sit there with pencil in hand completing math problems on a work sheet. In fact, it might take him an hour to do that. When you believe he knows the answers to the problems, it also becomes frustrating to Mom when he is still working on the same work sheet forty-five minutes longer than expected. I encourage parents to consider their goal. If you want Jacob to memorize his math facts, a work sheet might not be needed. Instead, ask Jacob to answer all the math facts out loud. This will take a lot less time out of your day than continually checking back to see if he has completed his paperwork, and you will find out immediately if he knows the answers or not. So in other words, take advantage of the fact that you are homeschooling and do subjects orally when possible, especially with younger students, reluctant readers, or students with learning setbacks.

If you prefer to think about how much time to spend on each subject, here is another guide you can use:

- Math—45 minutes per day (including speed drills for about 5 minutes per day), much less for younger grades

- Handwriting—20 minutes per day, but make sure your child has the fine motor skills to do handwriting without becoming overly frustrated; some children are ready at age six, others are ready at age ten

- Spelling—20 minutes three days per week, plus student must study for weekly spelling test

- Phonics—daily work for students learning to read with frequent, short sessions of about 10 minutes each

- Grammar—one or two days per week, 25 minutes per session

- Composition/writing—two or three days per week for older students; as much time as needed to practice writing and polish skills

- Reading—daily, as much time as student wants (chapter 7 includes suggestions on how to encourage reluctant readers)
- History—three days per week, supplemented with movies about historic events and field trips to historic sites in area
- Science—four days per week plus experiments at least once per month for younger and middle grades
- Geography/map skills—one day per week
- Art—one day per week; twice per month at local arts center
- Music—one day per week
- Computer—daily
- Physical education—at least 30 minutes of exercise daily (includes vigorous play or chores that require physical activity)
- Health and safety—integrated into regular discussions with child; daily health habits (such as brushing teeth)
- Bible—approximately 30 minutes daily
- Foreign language—15 minutes per day for younger students; 1 hour per day for older students

ONE-ON-ONE INSTRUCTION

One of the best things about homeschooling is the one-on-one instruction that is possible. This can mean providing individual help with a math problem, working with your daughter to ensure that she understands the phonics sounds, or answering your son's question about a word's meaning. As parents, all of us tend to be aware of

In middle school, our daughter began getting harassed. My husband was going to the school on a weekly basis. My daughter was headed in a direction that we were concerned about. She became very withdrawn, wanted to wear only black, etc. My husband and I decided to pull her out of school midyear. This was a very tough decision since we both work. We decided to undertake the task of shared homeschooling. He went straight night shifts while I worked during the day. He would sleep to noon, then homeschooling would begin. Then I would come home and finish. We divided the courses up based on our strengths. For the courses that we did not feel comfortable teaching, we used co-ops.

—Cathy O., Tennessee

our children's likes and dislikes, learning styles and abilities, making it possible to provide instruction that is catered to a particular child. Take advantage of this and enjoy all those times when you can help your child experience that "eureka" moment.

DAILY SCHEDULES

There are about as many daily schedules as there are homeschooling families. Just as many families prefer a flexible yearly routine, some families prefer a flexible daily schedule. This might mean that they don't follow any schedule at all or it might mean that they specify the day, but not necessarily the time, to study certain subjects. Here are some daily schedules with a flexible routine.

Family with biological children ages six, four, three, and one, and foster teens ages sixteen and seventeen

7:30	Mom and younger children get up when Dad leaves for work and drops off foster teens at school
8:00	Breakfast
8:30	Breakfast clean-up
8:45	Reading time with everyone
10:00	Playtime, then clean-up before lunch
11:30	Lunch
12:30	Lunch clean-up
1:00	One-on-one work with older child / quiet time for younger children
2:00	Get children ready to ride into town to pick up foster teen(s) from school
3:00	Outdoor play for children; Mom can catch up on chores or go outside with children
4:30	Mom starts preparing dinner
5:30	Dad arrives home from work; family has dinner together

6:00	Mom cleans up dinner dishes, vacuums, picks up toys, puts away books, etc.
6:00	Dad prepares children for bed, reads bedtime stories, gives baths if needed
8:00	Younger children go to bed; Mom and Dad spend time talking with or watching television with teens before bedtime at 10:00

Family with three children ages ten, eight, and four; Dad died last year, Mom continues to homeschool

7:00	Mom has quiet time alone, then wakes up children
8:00	Breakfast
8:30	Devotions
8:45	Everyone gets ready to do schoolwork (gather books, papers, etc.)
9:00	Older two children start written work where they left off during last lesson; Mom does pre-K program with four-year-old and helps older children as needed
12:00	Lunch
1:00	Rest time
2:00	Reading time
3:00	Everyone can go outside to play
6:00	Dinner
7:00	Children put away laundry, pick up toys, take baths if needed
9:00	Bedtime

Family with three high school students and one middle school student

- High school student one studies American history, biology, algebra I, and English I.
- High school student two studies world history, chemistry, algebra II, and English II.
- High school student three studies general science, basic math, and composition and grammar.

Marley homeschooled from the last half of third grade until the halfway point of sixth grade—while setting foot in twenty-two different countries. We spent all of 2008 in England. We were able to go to Paris and the beaches of Normandy, Amsterdam to see Anne Frank's house, Poland to see Auschwitz concentration camp, Shakespeare country in England as well as London and Stonehenge, and Berlin where we saw the remnants of the Wall. Our situation was very unique and homeschooling was what worked.

— Michael J., New Hampshire

- Middle school student studies geography, history, science, and pre-algebra.

Even though the students do daily devotions on their own, the family also has daily Bible study together. They also study Spanish I as a family. Each student takes weekly piano lessons and practices thirty minutes each day. The boys play basketball on a local homeschool team and practice a few times each week. The girl, age fifteen, plays volleyball with the local city league. In their state, the parents are able to apply Bible study and devotional hours toward elective credits; they count their sports activities toward physical education time, and piano lessons count toward music.

While the students do most of their work independently, Mom provides weekly lesson plans, and student work is checked once a week. As long as the students are working at a steady pace and keeping their chores done, Mom and Dad do not intervene.

Family with one daughter, age nine, with learning disabilities

6:30	Dad leaves for work
9:00	Mom gets up, makes breakfast (usually just pouring daughter a bowl of cereal), starts a load of laundry, makes bed, and starts dishwasher if needed
10:00	One hour of schoolwork, including about 30 minutes of reading time
11:00	Daughter has a break while Mom checks e-mail, reads news, etc.
12:00	Mom helps daughter do math
1:00	Break for lunch
2:00	One hour of work sheets

3:00	Life skills (clean, make her bed, discuss appropriate behavior, etc.)
4:00	Playtime outside with neighborhood children who are home from school, or she can choose to watch a movie until Dad comes home
6:30	Dinner
7:30	Evening television time together before sending daughter to bed; Dad and Mom usually go to bed around 10:00

Family with three children, ages twelve, five, and three

8:00–9:00	Mom and children get up, eat breakfast, and start doing chores (sometime between 8:00 and 9:00)
10:30–11:00	Twelve-year-old starts schoolwork; Mom cleans; younger children play
11:30	Usually an early lunch
2:00	Mom does history, science, and Bible study with all three children
4:00	Mom spends alone time with five-year-old doing phonics. Sometimes three-year-old listens in.
After dinner, children go outside and play or play a board game or cards before bedtime; Dad reads to children at bedtime	

Family with fraternal twins, age nine, and a ten-month-old baby

This family has a very relaxed schedule. They usually get out of bed when the baby wakes up each day, which could be anywhere from 8:00 to 10:00. They play together, read together, and take walks together. The nine-year-old twins enjoy riding their bicycles each day, taking care of their pet guinea pigs, drawing, and reading. They love it when Mom does science experiments with them. Both of the children enjoy cooking and playing educational computer games after their chores are done. Sometimes they do chores together and sometimes they split them up and take turns doing the not-so-favorite jobs, like cleaning the bathrooms.

We are more or less un-schoolers. I chose this style because it essentially meant not changing things. It's the way parents naturally interact with and educate their children before they are school-aged. I didn't really choose it so much as chose not to introduce any other kind of homeschooling.

—Aurore S., Switzerland

Mom believes that the most important thing she can do for her children is to train them to obey their parents and love the Lord. She also spends a lot of time with the children—showing them that she is interested in their lives and that she loves them. They read the Bible and also stories that contain character traits she wants to encourage in her children. Finally, Mom encourages the twins to spend as much time together as they want and also to play with and develop a relationship with their younger sister, whom they both adore.

For "school," Mom counts many of the twins' daily activities (chores, cooking, helping with the baby, taking care of pets, playtime for physical education, etc.) toward their state's required hours. When the children are interested in a particular topic, anything from ants to asteroids to word origins, Mom finds books on those topics and leaves them lying around the home or gives them to the children with a comment that she thinks they might enjoy it. This family's home is also filled with board games, puzzles, and educational toys. Mom has worked diligently over the years to make sure that their home environment is not only wholesome but also encourages learning, which means that the children end up doing much more than the four required hours per day.

When Dad comes home from work, he usually spends some time playing with the children while Mom finishes dinner. The family eats together, then they might watch an educational movie during the evening, and sometimes Dad will read a story out loud for the whole family to enjoy. Finally, Mom puts the baby to bed around eight-thirty, and around ten o'clock, the twins usually go to their room, where they grab a book or put on one of their favorite audio CDs (*Your Story Hour, Jonathan Park*, or *Adventures in Odyssey*).

Family with one son, age thirteen

Mom and Dad both work outside the home. Dad works mornings while Mom teaches writing and composition, logic, and history. Mom works evenings while Dad teaches science and math. Mom also takes son to co-op for Latin class on Fridays. Dad takes son to basketball practice with city league on Tuesday nights. Family spends weekends together.

Some families prefer more of a routine than a schedule. Below are some common routine alternatives.

Monday, Wednesday, Friday: math, science, composition
Tuesday and Thursday: history, Bible, spelling, and reading

Monday and Wednesday: all subjects plus housecleaning
Tuesday and Thursday: all subjects plus science experiments and
    music lessons

Monday and Friday: language arts, science, art
Tuesday, Thursday, and Saturday: math, history, geography
Wednesday: errand day

Four days each week: schoolwork from 8:30 until 3:30
Five days each week: schoolwork from 9:00 until 2:00 with one-
    hour break for lunch

Relaxed homeschooling: teachable moments throughout day
and year

In later chapters you'll find information about specific subjects and what counts as "education," volunteer opportunities, field trips, and social activities. These activities can be integrated into any of the schedules found in this chapter with only a little adjustment.

You'll also find information about how to make life skills part of your homeschooling routine.

WHEN ROUTINES ARE INTERRUPTED

Despite our greatest efforts, sometimes things happen in our lives that not only mess up our regular routines, but prevent us from fulfilling our usual household responsibilities. Disruption can occur after the birth of a child or if someone in the home becomes ill. You might need help as you transition to caregiver for your elderly parents or another relative.

Some people experience interruption to their regular routine for a short season while others experience interruptions more frequently due to situations like living with chronic illness. Regardless, there are going to be times when you might need to make practical changes to your lifestyle to preserve your sanity.

Meals

When something interferes with your regular routine, many things can be put off for a time, such as cleaning, schoolwork, and everyday errands. This does not apply to food preparation. After all, whether you pull a frozen dinner out of the freezer, order a pizza, or heat up a can of soup, someone has to prepare food for your family.

Normally our family eats very healthy meals, but since I deal with chronic illness, there are many days when we take shortcuts. I used to feel extremely guilty about this until I realized it was better for my children to eat instant meals than to eat nothing, or to be without a mom.

> My greatest stress has always been time management. There seems to be more to do than there is time to complete what needs to be done. While I still struggle in this area, I have learned that I truly cannot "do it all." I have learned that we must operate within a routine and a schedule, and at the same time leave room for the schedule to fall apart some days and not get too frantic about it. I have had to learn balance in this as well, and it is a daily process. What good is it if we finish a full day of schoolwork and keep the house clean and yet didn't have time to play together or sit together and talk? I guess I just try to keep perspective.
>
> —Rita C, Delaware

Here are some ideas you might want to consider if you experience a disruption in your home that is making it difficult for you to cook. Ideally, you'll plan ahead for some of these suggestions (like stocking up on frozen dinners).

- Don't be afraid to ask people to bring a meal when they ask how they can help. This is a huge blessing!

- If your spouse is willing, ask him to cook some easy meals while he is off work so that you can eat leftovers for a few days at a time.

- If you know in advance that you are going to be bedridden, cook several meals and store them in your freezer. Someone can easily heat them in the oven or microwave when needed.

- Stock up on frozen dinners, canned soups, snack bars, and other foods that can be prepared quickly and easily.

- When possible, put together chili, stews, or soups. These foods can simmer all day in a slow cooker and you'll have a meal at dinnertime.

Young Cooks

In addition to the above suggestions, many parents train their children how to prepare simple meals for themselves. Obviously this isn't something a five-year-old should do, but there are a lot of foods children can make by themselves. The great news is that you can even count this toward your required school hours since preparing meals is a life skill.

With minimal direction from Mom and a good stock of healthy finger foods in the pantry, even seven- or eight-year-olds can make their own snacks. Some of these foods may not be as healthy as what you normally eat, but many of them are.

- Sandwich meats, peanut butter, jelly, cheese

- Fresh fruit in season (grapes, blueberries, apples, bananas)

- Fresh vegetables (baby carrots, celery, cherry tomatoes, cucumbers, green beans, cauliflower, broccoli, bell peppers). All of these are easy to wash and can be eaten immediately.

- Canned pineapple, peaches, pears, mixed fruits

- Breads of all sorts (even if you normally bake all your bread from scratch, have some store-bought bread on hand in the freezer)

- Bagged salads

- Convenience foods, such as frozen dinners

- Crackers and cheese / packaged crackers and peanut butter

- Cereal

- Snacks such as wheat chips, pretzels, vanilla wafers, graham crackers, cookies, popcorn, tortilla chips, rice cakes, beef jerky

- Canned foods

- Boiled eggs

- Applesauce

- Health bars

Chapter 6

Extracurricular Activities,
Support Groups, and Co-ops

In recent years, as the ranks of homeschoolers have grown into the millions, homeschool groups and extracurricular activities have cropped up all across the United States and many other countries. Volunteer opportunities for moms and dads also continue to expand. The problem is that many families are so involved in outside activities that they are spending more and more time away from home. I believe this trend will eventually bring an increase of legislation for homeschooling and even a breakdown of the family unit.

All these activity options certainly help answer the "what about socialization?" question. But the pressure is strong for families to keep up with the Joneses and participate in as many activities, field trips, and other adventures as possible. Often the result is a very busy family with no real time to develop relationships in the home.

In this chapter, we'll take a look at the pros and cons of various extracurricular activities as well as homeschool support groups and co-ops.

ADVANTAGES AND DISADVANTAGES

The benefits of allowing your child to participate in extracurricular sports, clubs, and academic programs can be numerous. The child has an opportunity to play with other children, meet people with similar interests, and develop his or her skills. For older students, it is also advantageous for them to be able to list extracurricular activities on college admissions applications and scholarship applications.

> Every single moment in our daily lives, we learn and share in [an actual] setting . . . our home, the store, the library. . . .
>
> —Claudine A., British Columbia

> Activities give me time out of the house and I get to be with other friends. Plus, sitting at home working on schoolwork feels like it takes forever, but going out for activities makes my days more fun.
>
> —Garrett M., Maryland, sixth grader

As we've touched on before, there can also be disadvantages associated with extracurricular activities. Participating in organized activities and sports can be expensive. You might also be required to participate in fund-raisers to offset fees, uniforms, and travel expenses. Your child may also encounter people with very different beliefs from your own and he could be exposed to things you consider offensive. And finally, children—and parents—can easily become stressed if they have activities from morning until night. I've met homeschoolers who have been unwilling to take a day off for a picnic or other fun activity because they have so much scheduled that there is no time for a break (more on balancing the needs of your family later in this chapter).

FINDING THE RIGHT ACTIVITY

Extracurricular activities generally fall into four categories: sports, arts, service, and academic.

If your child is interested in participating in a sport, your options usually depend on what is available in your community. Homeschool groups in many cities are now large enough to have their own sports teams, but you may have to join the group in order to participate. Participation in a sport can be beneficial for any child, but for those who have a lot of excess energy, it may be just the thing they need to use that energy. Ask about fees up front.

Music lessons, art lessons, and drama classes may interest children who enjoy expressing themselves artistically. The fees for these activities can also quickly add up, so ask in advance for a disclosure of all costs associated with the activity. Don't forget to ask about art supplies or special clothes you'll need to buy for recitals.

Participation in service activities might actually be one of the least costly options compared to other extracurricular activities. Even young children can participate in service activities. This might include visiting a local nursing home once per week, baking cookies for the fire department, volunteering on a legislative campaign, or helping at a children's center. Just look around your community and you'll find plenty of people or organizations that can use a helping hand.

Academic clubs can be fun if you are interested in a specific academic area. While these clubs have traditionally been associated with public schools, you can form these clubs within homeschool groups as well. Or invite students from different homeschool groups in your region to participate. Start a history club, science club, foreign language club, or math club. See if you can find others who would be interested in meeting once a month outside of class to critique one another's creative writing.

GETTING INVOLVED

When you are deciding which activities your child should participate in, consider age stipulations, health issues, financial issues, the amount of time you will need to invest in this activity, and other requirements. For example, will your child need a physical exam and if so, will vaccinations or health problems be an issue? Also, many homeschool groups require that you be a member of the group sponsoring the activity before they will allow you to participate. Is it costly to join? If the group has a Web site, read their philosophy and see if you agree before becoming a member. Additionally, there may be religious requirements that you should consider. Do you agree with their religious philosophy; do they have a statement of faith? If the group allows open membership and you are not allowed to discuss religion, will this be a problem for you?

To find out about activities available in your area, check out the following resources:

- Local homeschool groups
- Area homeschool e-mail loops or Web sites (you'll usually find a lot of announcements about activities here)
- Recreation or community centers
- YWCA/YMCA
- Museums
- Libraries
- Boys Clubs and Girls Clubs
- Local agricultural extension service (ask about 4-H and other activities; some of these places sponsor classes on a regular basis)
- Bookstores (many bookstores sponsor card and book clubs)
- Churches
- Police athletic leagues
- Girls, Inc.
- Student flying clubs at the airport (many airports have flying clubs sponsored by local aviators or even military organizations; at our airport, students can join these clubs at age twelve).

Muddled Outings

Despite our best preparations, things can happen beyond our control—especially when children are involved! But I know from experience, God can bring good from perfectly messy, embarrassing situations.

Every family who falls somewhere between dysfunctional and perfect—in other words, normal—has most likely had an episode of shoelessness. Ours happened a year or so ago, after we had rushed to get to a doctor's appointment one morning. When we arrived and I opened the van doors for everyone to pile out, six-year-old Daniel asked, "Mommy, did you bring my shoes?"

Did I bring his shoes?!

After calmly explaining how generally we are supposed to get ready on our own—including putting on our own shoes—I announced he would just have to go in without shoes. My oldest daughter was mortified, but her brother did have socks on, and I couldn't very well leave him in the van. So I entered the building with two sick children, one shoeless child, one child fretting about germs, and one preteen walking at a distance from us.

It's tempting to see these "muddled outings" as setbacks. We fear that if others see us lose our temper or our child has a meltdown, people will judge us. While this may be true, worrying about what others think can lead to low self-esteem and decisions based on the opinions of others. Try to remember that some things really do happen beyond our control. And sometimes the good that results is as simple as a child learning to bring his shoes on an outing the next time!

For ideas on packing a supply tub for your car, visit *www.thehomeschooladvocate.com*.

SUPPORT GROUPS AND CO-OPS

I am hesitant to discuss homeschool support groups and co-ops because there will certainly be disagreement on this topic. For many, being part of a local support group can be the lifeline moms and children need to continue homeschooling. For others, these groups may replace or undermine the family structure.

More than likely there is a support group within thirty minutes of your home. If you're new to homeschooling, however, you may wonder what these groups are and how they differ.

A homeschool support group is just that—a group that provides support to homeschoolers. Smaller groups have five or six families, meet once a month for a playdate, and send out an e-mail notice occasionally. Larger groups have hundreds of members, sponsor homeschool sports teams, host curriculum sales, and sometimes organize co-ops.

A co-op is the term homeschoolers use to refer to "cooperative education." In a true co-op, parents pitch in and help out based on their own talents and desires. A homeschooling parent who has a degree in chemical engineering, for example, might teach a high school chemistry class. A homeschooling mom who enjoys sewing might teach an elementary sewing class. Another mom might volunteer to bring snacks every week for the members. In a true co-op, it only works if every parent is willing to help. If their child is participating, it is the parents' responsibility to find some way to contribute time or talent. In larger groups, there is usually a director who will help families find a way to volunteer if they are unsure how to help.

Some co-ops actually function as support groups. On a national

> Children are too busy these days. More unstructured playtime needs to be included in each day for the average kid to grow and develop normally.
>
> —Ellen D., Tennessee

> Great for the kids to have variety in co-ops and learn from others, but you can fall into the trap of going-going-going, and find that you neglect what you set out to do. . . . Educate your own children!
>
> —Michelle C., Pennsylvania

level, Jay and Heidi St. John of Washington State created First Class Homeschool Ministries to meet the needs of homeschooling families who want to participate in classes and group activities with other homeschoolers. While the St. Johns' ministry is designed to establish co-ops across the United States and elsewhere, the group usually ends up being a support group for homeschoolers as well.

SUPPORT GROUP ACTIVITIES

If you participate in a support group or if you want to start a new group, here are some of the activities your group may want to sponsor. Remember, these are just suggestions, and you might choose to keep your group small, without a lot of activities. That's not only acceptable, it has advantages.

- Moms' ministry, where more experienced homeschoolers mentor newer homeschoolers
- Moms'/Dads' nights out
- Moms'/Dads'/family retreats
- Family camping trips
- Sports teams (basketball, football, baseball, softball, volleyball, hockey, badminton)
- Swap Days, when families can bring things they no longer need or want and take things they can use
- Co-op classes
- Baby-sitting
- Clubs such as Girl Scouts, Boy Scouts, American Heritage Girls, 4-H, civic clubs, etc.
- Health fairs
- Field trips

- Curriculum/book sales
- Homeschool convention
- Informational meetings for people interested in homeschooling

CO-OP CLASSES

In a traditional school setting, teachers are limited in the things they can do and the types of classes they can teach. In a co-op setting, many classes are like semester or yearlong unit studies on a particular topic. Parents who are gifted in a particular area, whether science, foreign language, cooking, or whatever, can share their passion with a child much better than someone who has been told to teach a particular subject they have no interest in. Here are some suggested class topics:

- How to sew doll clothes
- Marsupials (or another animal)
- Economics for kids
- A specific missionary and where he or she served
- Study of a particular country (food, culture, clothing)
- Cooking (focus on ethnic foods, appetizers, desserts, or main course)
- Constellations (with a trip to a planetarium)
- World War II (or another time period)
- A specific character in a book, such as Kit from the American Girl books or Oliver from Charles Dickens' *Oliver Twist*
- A specific book or series of books over the period of the co-op semester
- Math games (fun ways to learn math)
- Phonics (for younger children)

This is only a small fraction of the classes you can teach; there are countless co-op classes and ways to teach those classes. The classes offered in a co-op are only limited by the imagination of the parents involved. As long as the parents are the ones doing the teaching and everyone understands that fees should be kept at a minimum, co-ops can be a wonderful way to introduce your child to other homeschoolers and expose him to different teaching styles. Co-ops also typically charge a fee, so at some point you have to decide whether or not the investment is worth the benefit.

CO-OPS WITH A UNIVERSITY SCHOOL MODEL

Some co-ops are not cooperative education at all, even though many homeschoolers still refer to them by that name. They are actually created from a university school model. This means that parents send their children to the "co-op," and paid instructors come in to teach the classes. Some places call these private schools or academies. Parents can leave and pick up the children later in the day, and the instructor typically gives assignments for the student to complete at home in addition to the work done in class.

In reality, I believe these university model schools or co-ops would be ideal for our public and private schools in the United States to utilize, as the benefits are numerous. Students can enroll in classes that interest them the most or in which they need help. Courses are

> Outside activities always seem to cause a crisis of belief for homeschoolers. Which ones do we need, which ones can we do without, and how much is too much? My opinion is that every family has to come to that decision for themselves according to their own convictions. We are very involved in our church, so the need for extra socialization is not really an issue for us. We began a co-op once a week when my two older children were in kindergarten and second grade and have been active in one every year since then. (They are now in fourth and sixth grade.)... I wanted them to have the experience of a more structured setting. At home, we do math on the floor in our pajamas, but I felt it was important for them to have the experiences of waiting in line, listening to another teacher, bringing necessary materials every week, etc.
> —Deborah C., Tennessee

taught by passionate professionals who have chosen to teach that particular topic. Students have the opportunity to fellowship with other students, learn in a classroom setting one or two days per week, and be exposed to the teaching style of instructors other than their parents. Many parents also like the fact that in these settings the instructors usually adhere to a schedule and demand that students do the same. These programs can help prepare a student who will transition to a public or private school setting or college. A student can be expelled from a class if his or her behavior is unmanageable, and students usually receive a grade.

One important consideration is the cost of these programs. Typical fees per course range from $50 to $150 per semester. For those who can afford this, it can be a wonderful option. For those with financial challenges, some university model schools offer semester-long payment plans.

BALANCING THE NEEDS OF YOUR FAMILY

Whether your child participates in sports, clubs, co-op classes, volunteer work, or whatever, make sure you watch for signs that your child or your family has too many obligations. If your child is not sick but he is excessively grumpy, tired, or uncooperative, it may be a sign that you need to pare down some activities. It is also easy to schedule so much that you neglect family time.

Volunteer opportunities, from one-time events to ongoing commitments, can sometimes add stress to a family rather than be a benefit or a blessing. For example, friends, relatives, church members, and others may assume that since a homeschooling mom is at home all day with her children, she has plenty of time to take on extra responsibilities. Some people don't know how to say no, so they agree to do things that they have no desire to do. When moms come to me about this issue, here is what I recommend:

1. Before you commit to any activity, tell the person that you will pray about it. This is essential. You should always seek the Lord's guidance before taking on more responsibility, but this also gives you a way out without having to say no right then.

2. Consider the amount of time the activity will require. Do you have time to help?

3. If you are married, what does your husband think? Will your involvement with this activity/commitment place undue stress on you or your family?

4. Are you helping simply because you were asked or do you truly have the ability/desire to complete the task?

5. If possible, don't commit to any outside activities until you have considered the above issues, spoken with your husband, and then spent even more time in prayer. If you pray about an issue before you tell someone you can't help, they are going to accept your answer a lot more readily than an instant no. If you are able to say yes, taking time to give your answer will also help everyone involved to be more comfortable with it.

The other problem with over-scheduling relates to what I mentioned at the beginning of this chapter. People are participating in so many outside activities that many families are spending very little time at home. In other words, they are spending very little time *homeschooling* their child. Sometimes they are filling their days with so many other activities that they do not have time to homeschool. Now, I'm a huge advocate of education outside the box. Learning doesn't have to take place at the kitchen table or with a specific curriculum, but at the same time, I see a growing trend of families who rely solely on co-ops and other activities to fill the educational needs

> There must absolutely be a balance, and at some times (when there is a new baby, for instance) there is not much that can be going on outside of the home. I would say at different times there is more time available to be spent outside of the house and at other times there is not as much time— seasons of life.
>
> —Theresa F., Pennsylvania

of their children. While it is possible for some children to receive a good education this way, parents would be wise to remember that we are told to train our children, and if we leave this to chance, we may end up with unsatisfactory results.

Any co-op leader will tell you that calls have increased dramatically over the past few years from new homeschoolers who want to put their child in the co-op "school." They think the co-op is going to take responsibility for the child's education, but co-ops are meant to be supplemental courses. They are not meant to replace the parents' training. In some states, parents aren't even allowed to count co-op courses toward the required educational hours. I think this is silly, but the thinking is that if the parent is homeschooling, then the parent needs to be the one doing the teaching. In other states, co-op classes are a welcome addition to the required educational hours.

> The main stress I see is simply trying to fit everything into the week. One of the ways we handle that is to schedule in time-outs, plan weeks off, plan ahead (much as I hate to do it), and the slow cooker is a blessing! It's such a little thing, but it really helps.
>
> —Bernie M., Australia

New homeschooling parents are enrolling their preschoolers in co-op classes at earlier ages every year. I received a phone call from someone last year wanting to know why I thought her son wasn't doing very well in his co-op settings. He was two years old and she had him enrolled in two co-ops each week! She told me that she needed that time away from him so they spent two days each week at the co-op. She volunteered in various classes and loved it, while her son sat in the nursery and cried. I told her that in my opinion, her responsibility was at home at this season of her child's life.

There are many such examples, but in general, homeschoolers are moving out of the home and closer to the institutional settings that original homeschoolers had hoped to avoid. If parents are supplementing with outside activities because the parent cannot teach that subject adequately at home, then the parent has taken responsibility for the child's education. The main thing to remember is to watch for signs that your child is over-scheduled or stressed. If you suspect that he is, make an effort to slow down and find ways to restore a healthy balance.

My first ministry is my kids, and I am able to say no without feeling guilty. My kids are more important, and a tired, stressed mom is not good for my kids.

—Tara B., Australia

Chapter 7

The Art of Academics

While it may seem that the average homeschooled child is appearing on *Good Morning America* because he was just accepted to Harvard at age twelve, your son is struggling to read and your daughter still can't say her times tables. Once you realize that your child might not be doing as well as his peers, you decide to buckle down and make sure your child is able to do all the things other children can do.

Our society places a lot of emphasis on early education, college education, high test scores, intelligence quotients, etc. Reading programs geared toward babies and toddlers testify to the fact that we are obsessed with how early children can learn to read.

With so much emphasis on academics, homeschoolers understandably feel pressure in this area. Unfortunately, in many cases, homeschooling families have sacrificed their moral standards on the altar of academic performance. In this chapter, we'll take an honest look at what this means for your family while you take into consideration your own preferences, chosen curriculum, and homeschooling methodology.

WHAT HAPPENED TO THE JOY OF LEARNING?

Ignorance is a handicap for everyone, and unfortunately we are producing more ignorant people in our society than ever before. We may have greater technological resources than any generation before us, but people have been swallowed up by these resources to the extent that we no longer produce the masterpieces of Mozart, Shakespeare, or Leonardo da Vinci. We use less of our brains and allow technology to think for us. This can be true for any student, regardless of his educational environment.

There are large numbers of people who are content to let others solve their problems, who have no desire to seek the truth, and don't seem to know the difference between right and wrong. As a society, it seems that we've largely focused on the answer rather than the process of getting there. In other words, if you have a calculator to tell you the product of 345 x 87, you don't need to know how to multiply without electronic assistance. If you can cheat on a test and receive an A, the important thing is that you don't get caught. There is a general mindset in society that says the important issue is the outcome. We are so busy getting everything *now* that we have lost the ability to focus on the *process* of learning as well as the outcome. The *process* of learning is largely what contributes to the *joy* of learning. Without the process as well as the reward of an answer, the joy is also lost, which is why many students in public schools, private schools, *and* homeschool settings have lost the desire to learn.

Of course, if all this sounds like doom and gloom, rest assured all hope is not lost! Many public and private schoolteachers are trying to reinstate hands-on education in classrooms, and if you homeschool, you already have the ability to integrate educational activities that bring joy through the learning process.

CHOOSING THE RIGHT EDUCATIONAL SETTING

Many parents do not realize that they have a choice when it comes to their children's education. If they can't afford private school, they automatically assume that public school is the only other option. In recent years, publicity has brought homeschooling into the public consciousness. Even though they are aware of the option, many parents still have no idea how to do it, and frequently the information given to them through school systems is incorrect. By the same token, some parents who have always homeschooled their child feel judged by other homeschoolers if they choose to put their child in a public or private school.

> When I put pressure on my daughter to perform well to please me, I know I am doing her a disservice because I am sacrificing her learning and self-esteem on the altar of looking good. Since I realized this, I have changed my yardstick.
>
> —Córee S., New Zealand

> I have taught in both public and private settings.... I do miss interacting with my students, but I love teaching my child the way I want him to be taught.
>
> —Jennifer S., Maryland

In reality, you are the best person to make the choice about the best educational setting for your child. Sometimes you might even need to make a decision for a particular child for a specific school year. So if you're trying to decide if homeschooling is right for your kindergartner, if you should send your homeschooled eighth grader to public school for the first time, or if you should bring your son home for his remaining elementary school years, hopefully the following questionnaire will help you make a decision based on academics as well as other issues.

Consider each topic in the following chart and then place a check mark under the school setting that best fits the description. I cannot tell you how to consider these. Some of your categorizing will vary depending on where you live or what you think the answer would be for your particular family or child. If you live in an area where your public school system has a good academic record, then you'll check that box. If you want to homeschool and you plan to provide lots of hands-on activities, then you should check that box. If the local public and private schools also integrate hands-on activities, then you'll check these boxes as well. Find out if the local public school actually provides time to explore private interests; measure the distance you would have to drive to private school; and investigate the costs associated with homeschooling—they're higher than you might think!

After you've filled out the chart, you can add up your results. Hopefully this will help you determine the best educational setting for your child. (You may want to use a pencil in case you want to reassess your child's educational setting later. If you've checked this out of the library, just make a copy of the checklist first or visit my Web site and print out a copy from there.)

HS = homeschool (all methods, including Charlotte Mason, Montessori at home, A Beka, or "unschooling.")

GS = government school/public school

PS = private school or Christian school (Use the PS box for whichever one you might consider.)

	HS	GS	PS
Academics			
Hands-on education			
Access to age-appropriate developmental puzzles and games			
Ability to spend more time learning material if child has not mastered it			
Ability to move forward if child masters material before other students			
Required mastery of material before advancing to next level			
Any subject that your child wants to study regardless of grade			

	HS	GS	PS
Access to humanities: art, music, etc.			
Mastery of a foreign language rather than minimal exposure with lack of fluency (If you want to homeschool, do you have the ability to teach this or access to classes?)			
Study of various scientific theories (evolution, creation, creation science)			
Historical study from original sources rather than or in addition to textbooks			
Ability to choose subjects studied			
Subjects out of order (chemistry before biology, for example) if desired			
Agricultural studies: farming, gardening			
Home economics: food preparation and care, how to design and sew clothes, homemaking skills, child care			
Other subjects important to your family (computer skills, gun safety, fish and game skills)			
Access to equipment such as microscopes, computers			
Time to explore private interests			
Freedom to read books not on assigned reading lists			
Socialization			
Access to a variety of people other than same-age peers			
Opportunity to travel throughout year on school days (Some private schools allow this. Most public schools do not. If this is important to you, ask before checking these boxes.)			
Field trips			
Ability to participate in clubs and activities			

	HS	GS	PS
Ability to participate in sports			
Exposure to team/group activities			
Cost (Factor in tuition costs for home school, church-related, or umbrella schools, as well as private school tuition.)			
Books and curriculum			
Additional classes such as co-op classes, dual enrollment, tutors			
Educational supplies (pencils, pens, paper, backpacks)			
Specific clothing (latest trends, uniforms, dresses)			
Transportation costs			
Lunch costs			
Participation in extracurricular events such as dances, ball games, support-group activities			
Environment			
Exposure to mold and mildew			
Exposure to microorganisms like mono-nucleosis, influenza and the common cold (If your child is highly susceptible to illness, do you have the option to keep him/her away during outbreaks of sickness?)			
Exposure to lice (If your child is going to attend a co-op or a day-care program, this could be an issue, as would attendance at any public or private school setting.)			
Small teacher-student ratio			
Choice of learning setting—desk, table, under a tree, on the bed (If you're not sure—ask. Many public and private schools now offer children the option to move around throughout the day, so this isn't necessarily just a homeschool option.)			

	HS	GS	PS
Competition among students (Do you want this or not? Find out what types of competition are encouraged in other school settings and decide if this is a pro or a con for your family.)			
Cluttered			
Calm			
Distracting			
Noisy (Is your home too noisy to study?)			
Comforting			
Values			
Measurable quality time with family (Is there a half-day kindergarten option? Do you want more time with your high-schooler?)			
Exposure to alternative lifestyles (If you consider this a good thing and it's offered, check the box. If not, leave it blank. If you don't want your child exposed to alternative lifestyles and it's not an option, then check the box to mean no.)			
Tolerance			
Religious instruction			
Prayer time			
Sex education			
Freedom to determine books and curriculum based on content			
Freedom to disagree with teachers and/or administration			
Students are taught moral absolutes			
Biblical worldview			
Secular worldview			

	HS	GS	PS
Humanistic worldview			
Students are held accountable for their actions (cheating, lying, stealing) (This may depend on your school system or principal. Ask what the policies are at your local public and private schools.)			
Students learn to respect people of all cultures, backgrounds, and religions			
Ability to opt out of programs or services based on moral or religious objections			
Parents are aware of educational content before it is presented to students, whether it is from books, lectures, or teacher opinion			
Parents have greater control over student's exposure to negative outside influences			
Develop and then encourage respect for authority			
Ability to seek other children with whom your child might develop friendships based on habits, hobbies, morals, and lifestyles, and filter those friendships based on parent preference			
Instill a positive work ethic			
Develop a sense of responsibility (chores, studies, community service)			
Celebration of holidays such as Halloween, Valentine's Day, St. Patrick's Day			
Celebration of religious holidays such as Good Friday and Christmas			

WHO'S RESPONSIBLE FOR EDUCATION?

Now is a good time to discuss a topic that's basically ignored in modern-day circles, but it's perhaps one of the most important things you can consider as you begin to homeschool. It's the burden of education. Who has the burden of making sure your child is educated? Is it the state, the federal government, you, your relatives, or someone else?

Before compulsory attendance laws, not only did children have a clear understanding of the moral code, but they grew into adults who wrote some of the greatest manuscripts known to man, composed beautiful music, produced magnificent works of art, spoke at least one or two foreign languages, and so on. Today, more than ever before in history, we have more access to books, teachers, and technology, yet we are sorely lacking in morals and academics! So how did people learn so much before we had institutional schools?

Before the mid-1800s, the burden of education was not on the government. Nor was it on the parents, other relatives, or the local superintendent's office (which didn't exist). The burden of education was on the individual! Yes, I'm talking about the individual child. Before compulsory attendance laws, children typically learned at home under the tutelage of their parents or, sometimes, paid tutors, until they were around twelve years old. Then, if the parent could afford to send the child to school, he entered a formal school setting and studied diligently for about four years. When the student was ready, he either entered a college situation or began working at a job. Regardless of who helped him learn, parents (and others) made it clear to the student that if he wanted to learn something, it was his responsibility to study, not their responsibility to teach.

Students knew that the burden of education was on *their* shoulders. If they wanted to learn something, they borrowed books or found someone who could teach them what they wanted to know. Education was considered a privilege.

I believe one of the main reasons homeschoolers and private school students do so well is because their parents have to pay for the education. It is not a free ride.

There are some homeschooled students, however, who refuse to do their work, and their parents are stressed out trying to ensure that they receive an education. Here are some ways parents can break that cycle and put the burden of education back on the student's shoulders.

First of all, too many parents waste time arguing with their children, threatening them, begging them to do their schoolwork. Instead, talk with your child and discuss his goals—short and long term. Determine the best ways to accomplish those goals, making sure you have the appropriate resources. Then place the burden of responsibility on the child's shoulders. This placement of responsibility worked for centuries and was obviously successful.

If our children are meeting our goals for them, I don't have to feel pressure to fulfill someone else's expectations for them.

—Hilary L., Singapore

Don't expect perfection, expect that they apply themselves.

—Lisa A., Oklahoma

Quite honestly, I don't teach my own children very much, but they do well enough academically because they have learned to shoulder the responsibility for their education. Obviously I've covered the essentials, such as teaching them to read and doing simple math—but beyond that, I've told my children that if they do not want to be ignorant when they grow up, they need to discover their gifts, find ways to use them, and prepare themselves for whatever it is they want to do in life. It is my responsibility to make sure they have the tools necessary to accomplish their goals, but it is their responsibility to study.

When your child takes control of his or her education, this doesn't mean you throw discipline, structure, and guidance out the window. It simply means that you allow your child to be the one responsible for his education. You may choose to continue with a schedule. You will want to guide him through Bible study and discipline. You'll want to answer your child's questions and provide good quality reading materials and other resources. You might even choose to have a structured curriculum. But do not waste time every day arguing with a child about doing his schoolwork. If he is not willing to do his work, tell him that is his choice, but he also cannot enjoy free time until he has done whatever it is that you have assigned (whether it is chores, a math page, a science project, or a book report). Then let him make the choice to be bored or to learn something. It will take time to see the burden of education shift to your child's shoulders, but be patient and eventually you will see positive results.

EDUCATIONAL RESOURCES

In a home where a child is going to bear the responsibility for his own education, it's wise to have a good collection of educational resources.

No matter what homeschooling method you use, the primary educational resource that I would recommend is a collection of great books. I love libraries, but we prefer to own our books so that we don't have to filter out books with content we would find objectionable. If your child tends to gravitate toward inappropriate materials at the library, but you don't have the money to purchase your own books, perhaps you should check out books you think your child would like while your child stays home with Dad.

A collection of good resources should also include art and music supplies, science equipment, maps, globes, rulers, and educational games and toys.

If you own a television, make an effort to collect educational movies, family-centered movies, documentaries, or other videos or DVDs that you consider appropriate for your family. If left to decide on their own, most children would watch mindless programming. If you set even minimal parameters, however, and allow one hour of television per day from the choice of any movie in your collection, and you already know you have only educational movies, then even during that free time your child will be learning something.

I have a huge list of resources on my Web site. Visit *www. thehomeschooladvocate.com* for a list of age-appropriate educational books listed by subject and reading level. There are also suggested curriculum lists, a list of educational games, and other resource suggestions. You can also find some of these in *The Homeschooler's Book of Lists* (Bethany House 2007).

IS ANY KIND OF READING GOOD?

Have you heard parents say they would rather see their children reading a "bad" book than not reading at all? Perhaps you've said this, and that's okay! But let's look at it from a food perspective. What if we said, "It's better for them to eat brownies all day than not to eat at all." No, not really. We're not talking about substituting one day's healthy meal for junk food. We're talking about a regular diet of brownies. So when it comes to reading bad books on a regular basis, you're talking about a regular dose of trash pouring into your child's heart and soul. In the next few sections, we'll look at some alternatives to "bad" books and suggestions on how to turn a reluctant reader into one who loves books.

When people say they are concerned about their children's reading material, I wonder who provides the books. If the parents are the ones providing the books, then don't they make the decision about what's appropriate and what isn't? If the child is making poor choices at the library or at a bookstore, then perhaps you should get the books until your child learns to make wiser choices.

If you tell your child that she can't eat brownies all day every day and you provide nutritious alternatives, she will eventually eat what you provide. If you start your child out with good quality reading materials, she'll be used to that from the beginning, but if you're trying to change bad habits (or poor preferences) that have already been established, it may take more time. Eventually your child will learn to use more discernment and choose appropriate reading material.

Put forth the time and energy to purchase good books for your child. Weed out the mediocre ones. Just get rid of them! Good-bye!

Don't give it a second thought! Then make sure you purchase good-quality books that promote a positive, biblical worldview that your child will enjoy.

WHEN TO BEGIN READING LESSONS

Despite the push for early reading skills, most homeschoolers have begun to suspect that it might be best to wait until a child is ready to read before starting formal reading lessons. This idea has been promoted by home-school pioneers and authors like Raymond and Dorothy Moore (*Home Grown Kids* and *Better Late Than Early* [with Dennis Moore]). The Moores and many others advocate allowing a child to develop naturally, experience lots of hands-on activities, and follow his interests. They further encourage parents to follow the child's cues when it comes to learning to read and starting other formal schooling. The following information will help you know if your child is ready for reading lessons, but if you want additional information specifically related to why parents should wait until a child shows signs that he is ready to read, I would recommend reading the Moores' books mentioned above.

> Our desire has always been that our children love the Lord with all their heart, soul, mind, and strength and walk in his ways. Unfortunately, in an attempt to ensure they were well prepared academically, I wonder if at times I deemphasized our spiritual priority. Although we praise the Lord that all of our offspring have accepted Jesus, we are disappointed that some have not wholeheartedly embraced our values.
>
> —Gordon M., Tennessee

Ready to Read Cues

Whether your child is three or nine, there are several signs to help you know when your child is ready to read. Does your child:

- try to sound out words
- copy letters, words, and symbols she sees written on something
- write letters

- write letter combinations (ARBL or hsC24kS) and ask you what they say
- ask you what words say
- ask you to read to him
- memorize short books and "read" those back to you
- "read" to her dolls, pets, or younger siblings

Notice that when children write letter combinations, they might use capital letters, lowercase letters, numbers, or even symbols. They might expect that the combination of several of these characters will make a "word" that you can read. After all, when you read to them, they see a bunch of characters together on a page and you make sense of it. They think that if they put the same characters together, you should be able to read those as well. Since young children still have the idealistic view that parents are perfect, you can have fun with them and make them feel good about their "words" by trying to sound them out. In other words, "ARBL" would become "Aahrbull." Non-readers find this great fun to see parents "reading" their new "words."

If your child is exhibiting several of the cues listed above, then you can be proud of yourself for introducing your child to the world of reading! These skills indicate that children have been introduced to books, written material, and reading. They see reading and writing as a normal part of life and have developed a desire to copy those around them. They want to learn how to read too!

One of the biggest temptations of new homeschooling parents is to fret when their child has not yet started reading by the age of seven or eight. Considering the fact that reading is probably the most important academic task to master, this fretfulness is understandable! Reading opens up a whole new world. It is also beneficial for parents since children can pick up a book and learn on their own whether you're sick, take time off schoolwork to care for a newborn, help your husband with a home business, or just need a break from teaching. On the other hand, spending day after day helping a child with reading curriculum when she isn't ready is frustrating for the student and the parent. Instead, consider spending that time reading aloud to your child each day, and when she shows signs of reading readiness, then start the formal reading lessons.

RELUCTANT READER TO BOOK LOVER

Studies show that by the third trimester, babies in the womb can hear and will even respond to sound such as a mother's voice. While most of us neglected to realize this and therefore didn't start reading to our children until much later, what's important to note is that sound is such an integral part of how children learn that they start using this ability before birth.

> I highly recommend reading to the children all that you can! Introduce them to all types of books. They learn lots and gain a love for reading and learning that way.
>
> —Nancy W., Oklahoma

Other than character issues, reading is the most essential element of a successful home school. The child doesn't have to know how to read, however, in order to benefit from great books. Children can understand books read aloud to them at a much higher level than those they can read. In other words, your child might only be able to read Dr. Seuss books, but if you read J. M. Barrie's *Peter Pan*, your child will understand what you're reading just fine. Here are practical tips:

- Make reading fun for your child. There are books on every subject imaginable. Pick books that your child will enjoy.

- Read aloud to your child. You know this is a good practice, but did you know that you shouldn't stop reading aloud to your child when he starts reading? Continue to read books to first, second, third, fourth graders, and beyond. Vary the type of books you read, but don't forget to introduce books above their reading level as well so that they can continue to learn new vocabulary and hear good reading techniques.

Let them pick books for you to read and alternate with classics of your choosing.

- Treat books and reading as privileges. When your child throws a book or leaves it on the floor, take it away. Train your child to appreciate books. Forcing children to read books as a punishment should never be an option. Remember, you want your child to associate books with something good.

- Don't ruin reading for your child. Institutional schooling has become so ingrained in our thinking that many people integrate institutional methodologies into homeschooling, even if they don't work. An example of this is when parents make children read aloud to them every day. While reading aloud occasionally can help a parent assess a child's read-aloud skills, when parents make a child do this daily, it tends to make him hate reading. Consider using the above ideas and let your child enjoy reading, but don't make it a drudgery. When you want to hear a child read aloud, have him read a recipe card to you, a piece of mail, or even Bible verses during devotional time. Those are practical, necessary things that help the child feel that he is reading for a purpose, and you might find that he enjoys reading books on his own more and more. To encourage placing the "burden of education" on your child's shoulders, give him the opportunity to choose to read or do other work.

- Encourage bedtime reading. One way to do this is to assign a bedtime, but tell your child that he/she can go to sleep OR read in bed. This is not playtime and there can be no games, toys, or other activities on the bed, but the child can read, or look at books if he is younger. Even though you may have a child who doesn't turn out the lights until midnight, I assure you that your child will develop a love for books if you give him the opportunity to read and let him make the choice to do it.

OLDER STUDENTS

I mentioned this earlier, but if you are beginning to homeschool a child who has been attending a public or private school, I recommend two things: First, put away the school materials and spend time (days or even weeks) talking with your child, setting goals, purchasing educational materials, preparing for this new venture. Some people call this "de-schooling." I recommend this process when you pull a child out of a traditional school setting. The child will need time to adjust to being at home all the time, and as a parent-teacher, you can use that time to study your child's learning style, academic strengths and weaknesses, preferences, and so on.

Second, have fun together. If you are in a state where you are required to "do school" from the very beginning, then spend the first few weeks taking your child on educational field trips, watching educational movies together, listening to history tapes in the car, and taking him with you on errands.

If you pulled your child out of public or private school because you were concerned about emotional or behavioral issues, spend some time renewing your relationship with your child. Consider individual (for your child) or family counseling if necessary and focus on finding a curriculum that encourages the types of behaviors that you consider appropriate. Some curricula, for example, are designed around character traits or principles of biblical wisdom.

Also, read the next chapter, which discusses building a firm foundation. Does he obey you? Does your child know what it means to love others and put others first? Can your child read well? If you answered no to any of these questions, I would suggest that you focus on these issues first. For older students, obviously you're going to be doing some academic work as well, but if your ninth grader is reading at a third-grade level, it's not going to do a lot of good to tell her to read Jane Austen because that's what you're supposed to do in ninth-grade English. Start at a level where your child is comfortable and go forward from there.

LIFE SKILLS

One of my favorite benefits of homeschooling is that it gives parents an opportunity to help their children develop life skills. People were much more self-sufficient before the introduction of compulsory education laws in the mid-1800s. There were uneducated people who learned to read and write and do math as a result of these laws, but millions more people have now lost the ability to grow their own food, take care of their homes, raise children, read classic literature that contains vocabulary well above the average sixth-grade reading level, and make moral choices. Many homeschooling families have recognized this and they've made these skills part of their homeschool curriculum.

Below is a list of basic life skills that you might want to consider for your home school. Many of these can be integrated into regular daily activities, but for others, you may have to take a class or find someone who can teach you the skill. This is only a quick sample list. There are many other skills you might choose to teach your child. If you'll e-mail those life skills to me, I'll add them to an ongoing list of life skills available on *www.thehomeschooladvocate.com*.

- manners/etiquette
- household cleaning
- laundry
- cooking
- gardening
- telephone skills
- caring for children

- caring for animals
- paying bills
- writing a check
- budgeting
- driving and driving safety
- completing a job application

CREATIVE ACADEMICS

One of the questions I commonly hear from moms and dads is how to teach academic subjects in an interesting manner. Most people are aware of the basic school subjects (reading, writing, and math). Some states even specify which subjects must be taught. Many new homeschooling parents dread teaching their children subjects that they found boring in school. It's important to remember that even if the law dictates the subjects you teach, they don't usually specify the way that subject must be taught, so this means you can get creative with your teaching style.

Schools are institutions and they have to function as such. It is difficult to cater to the needs and desires of specific children when you have a classroom of thirty students, administrative rules, and the preferences of diverse sets of parents. With home education, the parent can choose how to teach each subject, and once they start teaching academics creatively, many parents actually discover that they like the subject.

Don't be afraid to integrate creativity and fun into your academic studies! There are so many things you can do to make learning fun. Books are great, as we've already mentioned, but there are many other

> Our most embarrassing homeschool moment happened when my very intelligent first-grade son and I were at the library. My library card was maxed out on books so we were opening a library card for my son for his books. As we stood in front of the librarian filling out the application for a new card, my son asked me in a quite loud voice, "What is my last name?" I whispered to him his own last name. Once again he asked in the same loud voice, "How do I spell it?" As homeschoolers, it didn't seem necessary to write our last name on work we were doing at home, but it became apparent that we do need to write first and last names on our work at home! That day we began.
> —Sherri S., Oklahoma

When I pulled my daughter out of school, I imagined a comfy-cozy loving home school where there would be lots of reading aloud as we snuggled on a sofa. I dreamed of designing brilliant unit studies that would have my daughter exclaiming, "MOM! You're the BEST! I just LOVE homeschooling!" It was going to be a real fun adventure! That was before the control freak in me reared its ugly head, and I sat down and listed all the subjects she would have to learn. I combined the best of Charlotte Mason's charter school subjects with those of the classical home school and I came up with a curriculum that kept us at the table from nine to five. Needless to say, by the end of the first year, I felt depressed and burned-out and wondered what had ever possessed me to homeschool my only child for whom I was mother, teacher, facilitator, coach, mentor, role model, and playmate! I think it's fair to say that I did not even come close to achieving my goals, so I changed my expectations!

—Córee S., New Zealand

wonderful materials that can help reinforce the things you are teaching at home. Here is a simple list of suggestions to consider:

- Audio stories and lectures
- Books on tape
- Historically based movies or videos
- Documentaries
- Educational games
- Interviews with elderly persons, war veterans, older relatives
- Maps
- Puzzles
- Internships

MEETING REQUIRED INSTRUCTION HOURS

It's frustrating for new homeschoolers who live in states with required "instruction hours" to understand how they are supposed to fulfill those hours with young children who barely want to sit still for ten or fifteen minutes at a time. While parents should adhere to state homeschooling laws, it's wise to remember that parents are the ones in the home deciding how to best use those instructional hours.

A long time ago I heard that "education" is teaching someone something they don't already know or helping them become more skilled with the knowledge they have. That definition has stuck with me as we've homeschooled our own children, and I use this as a basis for deciding what we count toward the required instructional time.

When you walk into a dark bedroom to find your boys hanging upside down from the bunk bed because they are pretending to be bats, that's educational time as they reinforce what they learned from the book about bats earlier in the week.

When your nature-loving teenage daughter writes a letter to the editor of your newspaper, protesting the removal of a one-hundred-year-old tree in order to build a new condo complex, that's educational time spent writing about social issues.

When your ten-year-old son builds a new Lego ship and then makes a drawing of it for his collection of "ship designs," he is developing fine motor skills, using art skills, and thinking about engineering principles.

Here are some other ideas about what can be considered educational and the subjects they fall under:

> When my ten-year-old son was overheard playing with his action figures and made up a story line that went along with our recent history lesson on ancient Rome, I knew that stuff was sinking in!
>
> — Michelle C., Pennsylvania

- Teach your kindergartner how to tie her shoes (life skills).
- Help a first grader learn how to clean his room (life skills, organization skills, home economics).
- Take children on a nature walk (science, physical education).
- Read books aloud to your child (language arts, vocabulary, comprehension, plus whatever subject the book is about).
- Allow child to stay up late reading (reading).
- Let child paint on an easel outside for a day (art, science/nature/weather).
- Teach your preteen how to do laundry (home economics).

- Allow child to help with family business (economics, business, social skills).

- Take teenager for driving lessons (driver's education).

- Bake cookies, make a cake, cook dinner (home economics, cooking, math if you integrate measuring, elementary chemistry if you integrate discussions about change from one material to another).

- Bible study (Bible, reading)

- Mow the lawn (physical education, social skills).

- Playtime (physical education)

- Explore the creek, build a dam, look for water creatures (science).

- Teen mission trip (Bible, social skills, geography)

- Design a Web site (computer, reading, typing).

- Help balance family checkbook (economics, finances).

I've included examples from various age groups so that you get the idea. In the lower grades in particular, you can literally do the majority of your schoolwork without opening a single textbook. I know, because we've done it! Some people refer to this as "un-schooling," but we don't adhere to true un-schooling methodology because we occasionally use workbooks, and also, while we respect the child's opinion in making choices about educational activities, we still believe the parent should be in charge. We refer to our approach as "relaxed schooling," where parents are considered the guides, but the child's interests, desires, and abilities are always taken into consideration.

You should check the reporting requirements in your own state, but in general, it's very easy to find a way to creatively incorporate daily activities into the homeschooling portfolio. For moms who tend toward perfectionism, getting creative is the key to maintaining your sanity. It's tempting to enforce strict schedules every day and compare your precious little blessing to other children, but if you can find a way to relax, keep the learning experience fun, and integrate teachable moments throughout your day, you'll both enjoy homeschooling much more.

FIELD TRIPS

Field trips are a form of creative academics. They can be one of the most rewarding ways to learn about something as students experience things firsthand. After all, if a student has the pleasure of visiting Mark Twain's boyhood home, *The Adventures of Tom Sawyer and Huckleberry Finn* is going to mean a lot more to him!

Since most people are aware of the most obvious field trips—historical sites, science museums, art museums, nature sanctuaries, flower gardens, historical buildings, natural wonders—here is a list of suggestions outside the normal range of options:

- television stations
- radio stations
- city transit system
- subway
- mayor's office
- city commission meeting
- fire department
- police department
- airport
- local sports team training
- electric/water department

While these may seem commonplace to adults, they aren't for children. Remember to look at life through the eyes of your child. Look around in your own area and see what would make a neat field trip. Search online. Ask other homeschoolers what field trips they have enjoyed.

Field trips can be counted toward instructional hours, but a little preparation and planning can help you make the most of these educational outings.

1. Plan ahead. Verify the hours of operation. We once went to Kentucky for the purpose of exploring some of the caves there, which we thought were open year-round. It turned out that they are open year-round with the exception of ONE week every year when they prepare for the Lewis and Clark Festival. Guess when we were there? If necessary, schedule the field trip in advance. This will be required for places such as television stations, radio stations, and the like.

2. Make sure everyone gets plenty of rest the night before. It's frustrating when you're on a field trip with cranky babies and toddlers. Since a lot of homeschoolers are used to sleeping late, it's a good idea to plan an early bedtime the night before. Don't doom your field trip to failure just because everyone's sleepy.

3. Get an early start so that you arrive early with time to spare.

4. Make sure everyone has plenty to eat before you go, and take snacks with you.

5. Carry a water bottle for each person. This is especially important if you're going to be doing a lot of walking, waiting, or standing in the heat or sun.

6. Send everyone to the bathroom before a field trip begins. When we arrive on location, the first thing we do is find a bathroom.

7. Tell your children what's expected in advance. Will they be

allowed to ask questions? Will they be required to participate in activities? Discuss manners and rules, if they apply.

8. Decide in advance how you will handle discipline issues. If your child misbehaves, try not to discipline her in public. Take her to a rest room to discuss punishment. If you're part of a tour or other group activity, politely excuse yourself and talk with your child in private. If necessary, return to your vehicle to discipline your child.

9. Thank your guide, employees, reporters, or whoever else might be involved in the field trip before you leave. Follow up with thank-you notes, preferably ones written by the parent-teacher and the students in the field trip.

It's also a good idea to take photos when you go on field trips since these can be added to your child's homeschool portfolio. And remember, whether you take a field trip with a homeschool group or just your own child, you represent the homeschool community. Your behavior and gratitude for the experience will likely influence the decision to allow future homeschoolers the opportunity to visit.

> I would say that I think you'll enjoy homeschooling more than [public] school because you don't have homework to do!
>
> —Micah K., seventh-grade homeschool student

DEALING WITH INTERRUPTIONS

It can be difficult to help your child maintain focus during lessons or keep everyone sitting quietly on the couch during reading time when the phone is ringing or visitors are dropping by unexpectedly. Here are some things you can do to avoid one of the biggest forms of sabotage to the homeschool household.

- Turn off electronic devices (cell phone, pager).
- Turn off the ringer on your phone.
- If you have an answering machine, turn down the volume

so you can't hear it. If you are expecting an important call, check the machine during breaks.

- Make friends and family aware of your schedule. When we used to follow a strict schedule of homeschooling from nine to noon, my mom always made sure she didn't call until after lunch. Most people will be respectful of this if you explain that this is your child's *school*time.

- Post a note on your front door asking people not to knock or buzz the ringer during school hours or nap time. There was a time when we had five children ages five and under in our home, so we taped over the doorbell and put a note on our door asking people not to disturb us. That may sound rude, but it preserved my sanity.

- Don't let the computer, particularly e-mail, chat, and computer games, interrupt teaching time. Work these things into your schedule, set a limit for how long you're going to spend on the computer, and set aside potentially upsetting conversations, or messages that require long responses, for later.

- Don't be a distraction to your child. For some children, it can be distracting for Mom to be walking back and forth with laundry, talking on the phone, or typing on the computer while they are trying to concentrate.

Chapter 8

Nurturing Your Child's Heart

It is amazing how a parent's everyday actions can influence a child's character development. I learned this lesson while trying to mow our lawn one day.

There was a time when we had three lawn mowers, and none worked properly. After several summers of wasting countless hours yanking start cords, we finally decided to give away the old mowers and buy a new one.

After getting home from the store, I planned to push it around the yard a few times to create blocked-off areas for our two oldest sons to mow. I made it around the yard just twice before the mower abruptly stopped with a horrible noise. Someone, despite repeated reminders to pick up their toys and other things from the yard, had left a large pair of shrub clippers in the tall grass.

Boy was I mad! My poor children stood there watching me lose my temper, unsure how to respond. I had one hand raised in the air and the other pointing to the mower.

"THIS is why we do not buy new things!" I exclaimed. "We have not had this mower five minutes, and because people do not pick things up in this family, our new mower is ruined! This is a travesty!" (In hindsight, I probably looked a little bit like Lucy of *Peanuts* fame.)

After a few minutes of ranting, my eight-year-old walked up to me. "Mommy, I need to tell you something."

"Does this look like a good time to tell me something?!"

"But I REALLY need to tell you something."

I finally relented and asked what was so important.

He looked down and quietly said, "Mommy, I am the one who left the clippers in the yard."

I still needed a moment to rein in my anger, so I motioned him across the yard. As he turned, I noticed he began to cry.

Just then the not-so-gentle nudge of my heavenly Father reminded me of my many transgressions over the years—transgressions much worse than leaving clippers in the yard. He also brought to mind all of which I had been forgiven.

I walked over to Christopher and hugged him.

"Christopher," I said, "I am upset about the mower, but I am so sorry for the way I acted and for telling you to go away. I want you always to remember that I would MUCH rather have you be an *honest* boy who leaves things in the yard than a *dishonest* boy who always puts things away."

You should have seen the smile on his little face. It was worth many broken mowers.

That day I was reminded of the many ways we can influence our children's character. It's not just about demonstrating good behavior in front of your children or teaching them good character traits. It's certainly not as simple as teaching them the difference between right and wrong or telling them what you expect of them. It's not as easy as buying good curriculum or providing the perfect homeschool setting. Developing good character is about taking the time to recognize and encourage it. If I hadn't taken the time to calm my anger and praise

Christopher for his honesty, he might not have been so forthcoming the next time. He might not have trusted me in the future.

INTELLIGENCE VS. WISDOM

Most parents don't think twice about the nature of intelligence. We all want our children to be smart. Unfortunately, people have largely forgotten that there is a huge difference between intelligence and wisdom. Intelligence is a measurement of the things you know. Wisdom is your ability to discern right from wrong and make moral choices. A wise person will follow God. An intelligent person may or may not.

In Proverbs, we read that "the fear of the Lord is the beginning of knowledge" (Proverbs 1:7). We live in a culture that no longer fears the Lord. Many people even deny that God exists. Yet it's right there in black and white: The beginning of knowledge comes with the fear of the Lord.

Even if you've had a different philosophy in the past, each day brings a new opportunity to make changes to your homeschooling methods. That's one of the great things about the freedoms of teaching in your own home!

At the beginning of the book, I said that I wouldn't tell you how to homeschool. There are so many different ways to teach children and still come out with talented, well-educated, polite individuals. On this one issue, however, it's difficult to waver, and I can't stress the importance of it strongly enough. When parents focus on academics without any consideration of wisdom, they are likely to end up with very smart yet foolish children.

OBEDIENCE

As parents prepare to begin homeschooling, particularly if they want to integrate biblical principles of wisdom, it is beneficial to consider the issue of obedience. After all, if your child does not obey you, it's likely that he is not going to obey others or God. It's difficult to attain wisdom if you don't know how to obey.

With a young child, you have the benefit of being able to apply these principles early on. It is simply easier to train a young heart. Even if they stray from your teaching later on, the Bible tells us to "train a child in the way he should go, and when he is old he will not turn from it" (Proverbs 22:6).

If your children are already in their preteen or teen years when you find this book or start to apply the principles of biblical wisdom, don't be discouraged. Rather, see this as an opportunity to work on some of these principles while your child still lives at home. Sometimes it's helpful for children, particularly teens, to understand that authority comes from their parents, but even parents have a higher authority—God. Based on the commandments that were given to God's people and have been recorded in Exodus 20, children are commanded to honor their father and mother. Even if your attempts to guide your child go unheeded, continue to be persistent and present biblical truths in a loving manner.

As you help your child learn obedience, make sure that he knows the difference between outward and inward obedience. The goal is inward obedience with a cheerful heart. Don't allow your child to develop a fake sense of submission. Is he truly submitting to your authority, or appeasing you because submission is what you expect?

Finally, remember that learning to obey is more important than learning the capital of Zimbabwe or how to multiply numbers! I meet parents all the time who are so proud of the fact that their two-year-old can recite the alphabet, but when the parent tells the child not to do something, she does it anyway. You can teach an obedient child new things, but it is very difficult to teach a disobedient child anything!

Stay the course even when you're having a difficult day—or week or month—and memorize Philippians 3:13–14:

> Brothers, I do not consider myself yet to have taken hold of it. But one thing I do: Forgetting what is behind and straining toward what is ahead, I press on toward the goal to win the prize for which God has called me heavenward in Christ Jesus.

PUTTING OTHERS FIRST

I saw an illustration once that showed how the world tells us to put ourselves at the center of a circle (the universe) and then serve people from inside the circle outward—self, friends/relatives, acquaintances, then strangers. It's a perspective that has given us a world full of selfish people. Christian families should live according to a different circle: God first, then others, then self.

> I think parenting—and homeschooling—has given me even greater awe and gratefulness with how patient and loving and generous our heavenly Father is with us, his children.
>
> —Martha B., Georgia

Don't forget to focus on sibling relationships during the homeschool years. It might be helpful to review some of the suggestions for nurturing positive relationships in chapter 3. When you help your child develop positive sibling relationships, you are preparing your child to get along with others in society. If he can't relate well to and love those in his immediate household, it will be more difficult to love those outside the home. The time you invest now instilling unconditional love and concern for others will serve your child well later.

SERVING OTHERS

One of the best ways to encourage your child to put others first is to make sure he has opportunities to serve others. He can serve others throughout the day by opening a door, helping a younger sibling with his lunch or with a math problem, even offering to do something he wasn't asked to do. When your child is ready, you can also encourage the development of a heart willing to serve through volunteer opportunities.

Some of the following volunteer options are simple, others involve more time and effort, but all are worthwhile.

- Help an elderly neighbor buy groceries (older teen with license) or carry in her bags (even younger children can do this).
- Brush animals at an animal shelter or just spend time with them (helps with animals' socialization skills).
- Pick up trash along the road (with a parent).
- Bake goodies for local police or fire department.
- Teens can help someone learn to read at a literacy center.
- Organize clothing and other baby products at the local crisis pregnancy center.
- Answer phone calls at the crisis pregnancy center.
- Play with children at the women's advocacy center (mature teens only, since the children may talk about difficult experiences).
- Offer to baby-sit the child(ren) of someone who can't afford child care.
- Wash someone's car.
- Do someone's (sibling's, mom's, dad's) chores without a reason.
- Collect school supplies from local businesses for needy children.
- Sort Christmas gift boxes during holiday season (Operation Christmas Child).

- Volunteer at the local library.

- Organize a blood drive.

- Collect, stack, organize, and distribute at the local food bank.

- Help deliver food with Meals on Wheels.

- Find out what opportunities are available for young people through your local Ronald McDonald House.

- Make homemade cards for sick children in the hospital (even young children can do this).

- Write letters to service members overseas.

It's not really important *what* you choose to do. The important thing is that you are helping your child develop a heart that is focused on serving others. Volunteer opportunities are a great way to do this.

NAVIGATIONAL SYSTEMS FOR LIFE

As you consider ways to nurture your child's heart, it might be helpful to know about a recent trip I took to Vanderbilt Hospital in Nashville.

A friend of mine was accompanying me on the trip. Before we pulled out of the driveway, my friend said that we were going to use her Garmin to navigate the way. I had never seen a navigational system before so I was eager to discover what it would do.

Sure enough, when we came to the end of my road, it told us which way to turn. Before we came to the end of the next road, however, we had to take a detour due to road work. The GPS system told us that we had made a wrong turn and when I didn't stop, it said, "Recalculating." After about twenty seconds, it said, "Go forward five hundred feet and make a U-turn."

I thought that was the funniest thing! We laughed until we cried.

This little electronic device was certain that we were going the wrong way because it didn't know about the detour. Of course, we would have reached the end of the road much faster, saved gas, and avoided several turns if we had been able to stay on the intended path. After the detour, we were redirected, and the GPS system was very useful for the remainder of the trip. It directed us to our destination safely and then out of Nashville in the most efficient manner.

As I thought about the usefulness of this tool, I marveled at how wonderful it would be if we had a Garmin for life. What if we started down the wrong path and we suddenly heard a voice that said, "Go forward five hundred feet and make a U-turn"?

In reality, we do have navigational systems for life—the Holy Spirit, the Bible, our conscience, godly mentors, books with a biblical worldview. I just love the fact that God loves us enough to provide us with our own personal Garmin!

FINAL THOUGHTS

On the whole, homeschooling parents do a wonderful job of sheltering their children from the evils of the world. As a matter of fact, this is a frequent complaint of critics—that homeschoolers are too sheltered. Despite the criticism, sheltering a child can have obvious benefits during crucial developmental periods. No matter what we do, though, we cannot take away the inherent sinfulness in our children's hearts. The Bible says, "Folly is bound up in the heart of a child" (Proverbs 22:15). We cannot keep children from sin, but we can guide them and train them and share with them the Good News that Jesus Christ paid the penalty for their sins when he died on the cross.

Chapter 9

Living in a (Very) Messy House

At times my focus needs to shift from being a homeschooling mom to a working mom who homeschools. For instance, when I'm facing a writing deadline, it's impossible to get everything else done, so I take a break from lessons and housework. There is no time to clean, everyone eats sandwiches or leftovers, and my evenings are spent on the couch with the computer on my lap.

As I was going over last-minute changes for this book, Micah and Sarah were nearby, so I asked their opinion of my chapter titles. After I read the original title for this chapter, "Living in a Messy House," I awaited their responses.

Micah looked around the room quickly and replied, "Um, Mommy, I think the title of that chapter should be 'Living in a VERY Messy House.'"

Somehow it helps knowing that every homeschool mom experiences times when she can't catch up on everything that needs to be done. Not only are we responsible for the normal daily activities of caring for a family, but we're supposed to spend a good portion of our time educating them as well. It's our responsibility to impart knowledge of history, science, proper grammar, foreign languages, math, and all the other academic subjects they need before graduation. That's in addition to cooking, cleaning, shopping, mending, nursing babies, being a helpmeet to our husband, chauffeuring family members to doctor appointments and soccer games, and the list goes on and on. All parents face challenges, and sometimes the tasks may seem daunting, but imperfectly balancing the many responsibilities in a homeschool family is normal.

Messiness is going to happen. And it's quite possibly worse for homeschooling families when you consider the following:

- Homeschool families typically spend more time at home, which means more opportunity to mess up the house.

- Even if you follow a relaxed form of schooling, there are likely to be books, curriculum, craft materials, and other education-related items in your home. Homeschoolers tend to have more materials like this than an average household, and these things create clutter!

- Many homeschool families incorporate chores as part of their child's "life skills," which means you have more help taking care of the household tasks, but your young helpers may not yet be efficient or thorough with cleaning tasks.

At times our house is incredibly messy and occasionally it's uncommonly clean. Frequently there is a frustratingly large amount of clutter all over the place. Often when we start cleaning, the children automatically ask, "Are we expecting guests?"

Of course, I've been in homes where there is nothing out of place and not a speck of dust anywhere. Like everyone else, I've had those fleeting moments of envy, wishing desperately that *my* house could look so good. (Well, perhaps they were longer than fleeting.) Still, let me warn you that if a perfectly clean house is truly your goal, stop reading now! You are not going to discover how to have a perfectly clean house in this book any more than you'll figure out how to make your kids behave all the time, pay off all your debt next month, or prevent your child from suffering. That being said, there are ways to make improvements.

CHORES

My children sometimes mention not-so-casually how friends are paid for doing chores or receive an allowance "just for being part of their family." The other day they told me a homeschooled boy we know is paid a good amount of money for mowing his lawn each week. They pointed out that he even uses a riding lawn mower. Our children have to use a push mower, and I don't pay them anything. They said it wasn't fair. I suggested a compromise: Since we have little money to spare, we couldn't pay them for regular chores, but we would start paying a small amount each week for mowing the lawn. (I also said they were welcome to save their money and buy a riding lawn mower!)

Most children go through phases of wanting to know why they have certain responsibilities. When they question doing chores, it isn't always a sign of rebellion. If you want to give your child a practical reason why you assign household chores, here are some benefits that you might mention:

> Our son is responsible for the dishes (including running the dishwasher) and taking out the trash every day, as well as keeping his room and play areas neat. If he performs his chores, he gets $1 per day. He can also make an extra $1 for each load of laundry. To date, he has well over $100 and prides himself on saving, not spending. Enforcement is simple. If he does not complete his chores and we have to do them, he pays us $1. He HATES this, and it's been strong motivation to keep him on top of his responsibilities!
> —Jennifer M., Maryland

- Chores make a child feel more a part of the household.

- Chores give a child a sense of responsibility.

- Chores help children learn life skills (laundry, cooking, doing dishes) that will help them later in life.

- When they do chores, children learn that it's not all about them. If they don't feed the dog, for example, the dog will go hungry.

- Chores help develop a child's pride in his or her surroundings.

- Chores help children learn that if they needlessly change into other clothes, carry dirt into the house, use too many dishes, it creates more work for someone in the home (preferably them if they created the mess).

Organizing Chores

Among the many methods of organizing chores, here are some that work best for homeschooling families.

Weekly Chore Chart: Keep a chore chart listing who is responsible for specific chores on particular days and then rotate the chores occasionally. We found that it helps to keep the same chores for at least two or three weeks so they can master the chores before trying new tasks.

Chore Calendar: Assign chores for the whole month on a calendar and keep it posted in a prominent location.

Chore Jar: Draw chores from a daily chore jar. This works well for children who need more stimulation or who have low attention spans. You can also use the chore jar as a supplement to other methods when you need to dole out punishment in the form of manual labor. Have the child draw a job from the chore jar and complete the task as a form of consequence. Normally I don't advocate training children to see chores as "punishment," but if you use it sparingly, manual labor can be an effective means of discipline.

Notebook: Have the child keep track of his assigned and completed chores in a notebook. If you are required to keep a portfolio of the child's schoolwork for the year, the notebook can be part of that portfolio.

Room/Area Assignment: Some parents make each child responsible for cleaning a particular area. Examples of room and area assignments appear later in this chapter.

Pocket/Card System: This is my personal favorite. It can be used for large or small families. The parent assigns the chores, and the student is responsible for checking his assignments each day and then letting you know that he has done them. It's an inexpensive system. You can purchase a chore system with pocketed organizers and pre-made cards that have a chore listed on each card by name. Some have pictures so that even young children can "read" the cards. Or you can make your own chore organizer based on the same principle. Here's one way:

> You'll need a piece of cardboard or card stock for the background. For the pockets, you can do something as simple as cut an envelope in half so that you create two "pockets" out of each envelope. Just cut as many envelopes as you need to create two pockets for each child. Put the names of various chores (laundry, dishes, feed pets, mow lawn) on small-size index cards. You can write these neatly with a pen or marker or print them on your computer. To make the cards more fun, some families let the children color the chore pictures on the cards.
>
> Meanwhile, divide the card stock into two sides so that there is one side for "to do" chores and the other side for "done" chores. Glue or staple one pocket for each child on the "to do" side and one for each on the "done" side. Label the pockets with each child's name. Next, you'll either need to attach magnets to the back of your background or add a little string to hang your chore organizer and display it in a convenient place. Put the chore cards that you made out of index cards into the pockets on the "to do" side as you want to assign chores. The child is responsible for

checking these each day, completing the chore, and then moving the cards to the "done" side. Your responsibility is to check the "done" pockets later in the day to make sure that the cards have been moved. (In the beginning, you may also want to check to make sure the chores are done to your satisfaction.)

Commercial Chore Organizers: Several wonderful chore organization systems are on the market, including those created by families who wanted a better way to organize their children's chores. Some were created to meet the needs of large families. Others are meant for families with one to four children, but you can order extra materials if necessary. Here are some suggestions for commercial chore organizers:

- *Managers of Their Chores* from Steven and Teri Maxwell. (The Maxwells have also written *Managers of Their Homes: Homeschooling with a Meek and Quiet Spirit,* and *Preparing Sons to Provide for a Single-Income Family.*)
- *Choreganizers* from Steward Ship Publishing
- *Clean N' Flip* chore organizers from Trigger Memory Systems: *Zone Cleaning for Kids, Bedroom Cleaning for Kids,* and *Laundry for Kids*

AGE-APPROPRIATE CHORE SUGGESTIONS

When parents assign jobs that are too difficult, it can frustrate the child and make him feel like a failure. Age-appropriate chores will help your child develop confidence and ability to complete chores efficiently. I first developed the following lists of age-appropriate chores for *The Homeschooler's Book of Lists* (Bethany House, 2007).

Helpful Hint

Many homeschoolers do not realize that chores can be counted toward mandatory "educational hours" because they are categorized as life skills, an essential part of any well-rounded curriculum—regardless of the educational setting. For example, when your five-year-old helps weed the garden, she is learning about nature, plants, and weeds, which all fall under the category of "science." Additionally, her work could count toward physical education time. If your fourteen-year-old cooks the evening meal, not only is she doing her chores but she is also doing math (measuring and planning portion sizes), home economics, and reading and interpreting recipes.

Chore Ideas for Toddlers

- Set table (plates and silverware—not sharp knives)
- Take dirty laundry (in small piles) to laundry room
- Dust (a feather duster works well for toddlers; avoid sprays, especially for children with allergies)
- Help unload dishwasher
- Take small bags of trash to trash can
- Help wash kitchen floor (with small rag)
- Wash front of cabinets, dishwasher, stove (make sure it's not hot), refrigerator
- Put their own clothes away (not including folding)
- Fold washcloths or other small items
- Pick up toys
- Check mail (with a parent)

Chore Ideas for Children Ages Three to Five

All of the above chores for younger ages, plus:

- Bring in groceries after a shopping trip
- Help prepare meals
- Help set table (including food dishes that aren't hot)
- Wash bathroom sink, floor, bathtub, and toilet (with supervision)
- Feed pets (such as fish, rabbits, or other easy-to-feed animals)
- Help take folded laundry to correct rooms
- Help get out ingredients to cook or bake
- Take items to other parts of the house
- Take a thank-you note or return a borrowed book to a neighbor (with adult supervision and not across a road)
- Take mail to box and put up flag (with supervision) or allow child to help take out and put mail in box at post office
- Weed garden
- Water plants
- Help make beds

Chore Ideas for Children Ages Six to Nine

All of the chores for younger ages, plus:

- Take out the kitchen trash and replace trash bag
- Mop kitchen floor (with mop or rags)
- Vacuum (depending on size and ability to use vacuum, of course)
- Dust

- Clean windows and mirrors with glass cleaner
- Wash dishes with help
- Help younger siblings fix bowls of cereal, bagels, other non-cooking type foods
- Play with or keep an eye on younger siblings for short periods of time while Mom cleans, does school, or rests
- Feed and water pets and smaller outside farm animals
- Change litter boxes (may need help to clean the whole litter box)
- Empty dishwasher (put away silverware—not sharp knives—and stack plates and cups on counter for Mom or older sibling to put away)
- Watch timer for items in oven and call Mom or Dad when they are ready (teaches responsibility and beginning cooking, but the child is not old enough to take items out of the oven without help)
- Weed garden (younger children could help with this, but they should learn the difference between a weed, a vegetable plant, or a flower)

Chore Ideas for Children Ages Ten to Twelve

All of the chores for younger ages, plus:

- Help Mom or Dad cook
- Begin to cook some items alone with adult supervision
- Empty all trash in house and replace trash bags
- Help sort laundry to be washed
- Load washer, add detergent, and start load
- Put clothes from washer to dryer and start load
- Unload dryer and sort clean laundry

- Help fold clothes
- Mow yard (could start a little younger, but either way make sure the child has constant supervision, as mowers are dangerous machines)
- Wash dishes without help
- Clean up kitchen after meals
- Help groom animals (brush cats, dogs, horses; clip nails)

Chore Ideas for Children Ages Thirteen to Fifteen

All of the chores for younger ages, plus:

- Watch younger siblings at home alone for short periods
- Cook meals without supervision (an adult should be in the house, however, in case of emergency)
- Do laundry alone (from washing it to putting it in rooms to be put away)
- Take trash and recyclable boxes to roadside
- Be fully responsible for care of animals (feeding, cleaning, grooming)
- Help with paperwork (depending on family preferences for allowing this sort of work, child may be able to complete forms, write checks, pay bills)
- Take care of household chores and take on neighborhood jobs, if desired
- Use edging trimmer (with supervision)

ROOM/AREA ASSIGNMENT SUGGESTIONS

Some families choose to assign chores by area of responsibility. This particular method works better for larger families if you want to make sure every room in the house is assigned to someone. You don't want to overwhelm one or two children with the responsibility of a huge area to clean each week. On the other hand, if you have several children, this is a great time to point out that more helpers means lighter work or less work for everyone. It's a simple division problem, so you can incorporate a little math as you make room assignments.

Parents will need to decide which chores should be done on a daily, weekly, or monthly basis. Some chores, for example, such as loading or unloading the dishwasher, could potentially need to be done daily or even a couple of times per day. Other chores, such as making sure soap dispensers are clean and filled, may need to be done only once per month.

> **When you are a part of a family, it is expected that you have responsibilities because you are a part of the team and not because you are expecting something in return.**
>
> —Jacqui H., Indiana

The following cleaning assignments are suggestions for each room based on an average homeschooling household. You'll notice in the dining room, for example, that I have "organize bookshelves" and "sharpen pencils." This is because many homeschooling families keep their homeschooling supplies in the dining room. Just amend the list so that the chores fit the rooms and the children in your own home. Also keep in mind that these are suggestions. Design a plan that works for your family.

Kitchen

- Load and unload dishwasher
- Hand-wash dishes that won't fit in dishwasher
- Wipe down counters and stove top
- Wipe front of refrigerator and other appliances (occasionally or as needed)
- Clean inside microwave when needed
- Take out trash and recyclable items

Dining Room

- Clear and clean table
- Push in chairs
- Sweep and mop or vacuum
- Dust
- Organize bookshelves
- Clean windows
- Sharpen pencils

Bathroom

- Wash sink
- Clean mirror
- Wipe down shower or bathtub
- Clean outside and then inside of toilet
- Sweep and mop floor
- Fill soap dispensers when necessary

Laundry Room

- Gather all laundry from bathrooms or laundry buckets (Many families make each child responsible for their own laundry, but we assign this task separately.)
- Sweep and mop floor

Living Room

- Make sure things are put away
- Organize bookshelves
- Dust

- Wash windows as necessary
- Wipe mini-blinds (occasionally)
- Add water to humidifier
- Vacuum (occasionally pull out couches and chairs and vacuum under them and under cushions)

Pets

- Feed and water pets
- Brush animals each week
- Make sure animals have no injuries that need to be cared for

Yard and Porch

- Put away toys
- Walk around yard and pick up any windblown debris
- Gather broken branches
- Mow lawn (older children)
- Sweep porch
- Make porch presentable as necessary (put things away, reorganize chairs)

SEASONAL CLEANING

Some chores are best done on a seasonal basis. We have found it helpful to create a separate list of spring chores and fall chores.

> In our early years of studying grammar, we learned that *dust* can be a noun as in "the dust is thick on the furniture" or it can be a verb like "next week we will dust." For this season of my life, it is usually a noun. Once or twice a year it is a verb.
>
> —Laura W., Tennessee

Spring Chores

- Bring out spring/summer clothes. If you aren't sure if something fits, try it on as you pull it out! It's a waste of time and space to put clothes that are too small in your drawers or closet.

- Once the weather is warm enough, pack away winter clothing that will fit next year, and decide how to discard winter items you will not keep. Give them away, sell them online, or donate them.

- Look through curriculum from the previous year. If you're finished with it, decide if you'll sell it, donate it, or keep it for future use.

- Change all air filters.

- Check light bulbs to see if any need to be replaced.

- Walk around your house and yard and make note of any repairs that need to be made.

- Wipe down outdoor furniture.

- Schedule a day to clean out the garage, attic, or cellar. Plan a yard sale if necessary. Better yet, read the next section on downsizing and do that in the spring.

- Scrape, prime, and paint any outdoor areas of trim or woodwork that need to be repainted.

- Prepare garden for planting. Plant when the time is appropriate.

- Check gardening guides to see if your bushes or trees need special care during this time.

- Check outdoor animal cages/shelter to see if they need any repairs after winter weather.

- Clean windows inside and outside your house.

- Inspect your air-conditioning system or arrange for a technician to do it.

- Either take your automobile in or do a checkup yourself.

Have your tires rotated and balanced, change the oil, change the air filters, make sure fluids are topped off.

- Wash your automobile and remove any undercarriage salt sediment that may have been pushed up from winter roads.

- Go through school-related papers for the previous year. Throw out excessive paperwork and file what you need to keep.

Fall Chores

- Organize homeschooling books and curriculum.

- Make sure you have the supplies necessary for upcoming academic projects. (It's easier to plan ahead and do this with your other chore activities; then you'll have what you need when you need it.)

- Bring out fall and winter clothing. Try on clothes and get rid of things that no longer fit.

- Make sure each family member has everything they will need for the next two seasons (fall and winter) so you're not stuck without a winter coat or long socks for a family member.

- Inspect heating system or arrange for a technician to do this.

- Change air filters in the house.

- Clean leaves and other debris out of gutters.

- Check outdoor animal cages/shelters and make any adjustments in preparation for cold weather.

- After you've harvested your fall garden, either plant a cold-weather garden or prepare your garden for the spring.

- Check gardening/plant guides to see if any of your other outdoor flowers, shrubs, or trees need special care during this season.

- Clean windows inside and outside your house.

TOYS

It hardly needs to be said, but in most homes with one or more children, the number one contributor to messiness is toys! Can you relate? It's a particular problem in our society where children have too many material items, including toys. There are several things you can do, however, to avoid toy clutter.

One way to combat this problem is to purchase gifts that will benefit the entire family, such as a museum or park pass. These make nice gift ideas for friends or relatives who might want specific suggestions of things your child (or family) might like. In situations where you want to purchase something for an individual child, consider purchasing gifts such as tools, sewing supplies, riding toys or bikes, books, and balls and other sports equipment. These things will last much longer than the average toy and will contribute to the child's educational endeavors.

> **People who like perfectly clean homes should not homeschool!!!**
> —Siggi H., New Zealand

> **You just need to get used to the idea [if you home-school] your house is not going to be perfect.**
> —Theresa F., Pennsylvania

If there are miscellaneous toys your child wants to keep that don't belong with a set, put these in one single toy box that everyone has access to. Your own child and his friends can play with the items from this box, and if you have one place to store all of these miscellaneous toys, everyone will know exactly where the items need to go when they play the "clean-up" game.

We also encourage the purchase of "sets." Our children love to play with Playmobil, Legos, Lincoln Logs, K-Nex, and other creative toys. They re-create wars, design entire communities, and pretend to be in a different time period or location. Creative toys encourage pretend play and role playing. Sometimes we do read-alouds while our children are playing with these types of toys. It fosters the child's imagination.

I've heard many parents say their children leave toys with small parts lying all over the place and won't pick them up. It's an old trick, but we rotate the sets so the children don't become bored with the set that's out. We keep our sets in our storage area and bring out one set at a time. We'll leave it out for a couple of weeks, and then put it away again. That way the toys are more interesting when we bring them out, and the children seem to appreciate them more. If the kids won't pick up pieces, they argue over the parts, or don't seem interested in the set, we put it back in storage for a while.

BOOKS

For many homeschooling families, including ours, books are invaluable. We derive great pleasure from all the different books in our home, but they are also our biggest source of clutter. When the children were younger and our book collection began to grow, I decided that we had better do something to organize them or we would have no idea how to find a particular book when we needed it. The system, which we still use today, is similar to the Dewey decimal system you'll find in libraries, but with a few adjustments tailored for a homeschooling family. Now when we want a book, we know where to look. (Well, most of the time!)

Despite times when things are not (quite) organized, it's still helpful to have a general idea of where the books should go so that when you have time to clean or when you want to read a particular type of book, you'll know where they're supposed to be. Since many homeschoolers' lives largely revolve around books, it's very helpful to have them at least somewhat organized so that you don't waste time looking for a book about Egyptians or wasps or whatever topic when you need it.

We maintain a small area for adult fiction. These are alphabetized by last name of the author, but the children have to ask permission before they can read these books. We do let them read some adult fiction and we don't have anything "bad" in our home, but we want to make sure a child is mature enough to read something such as *The Plague,* by Albert Camus, or *The Lord of the Rings,* by J. R. R. Tolkien. With the exception of the adult fiction books, the children can read the books in our home any time they want to.

Juvenile fiction books are also alphabetized by last name of the author.

Adult nonfiction books are all located in the same area. They are organized by topic, but we have very few of these. The adult nonfiction books we do have pertain mostly to homeschooling, parenting, or financial freedom.

Juvenile nonfiction books are organized throughout the house by topic. Here are our sections:

- Math books include anything related to math topics, such as money, curriculum, math game books.

- Science books include curriculum, nature guides, and anything else related to science. The books are organized by topic, including nature, animals, stars, creationism, evolution.

- Religious books include books about Christianity as well as other religions. There are Bible studies, Bible verse memorization cards, and various translations of the Bible.

- Language arts books include curriculum, workbooks, and activities that encourage language arts, such as Mad Libs. This is one of our smallest sections because we believe children learn language arts through great literature, whether they are reading it or having it read to them.

- History books are organized according to the various time periods up to the modern day.

- Biographies are in alphabetical order by the last name of the subject. There are also sets, such as CHILDHOOD OF FAMOUS AMERICANS and YWAM's CHRISTIAN HEROES series by Janet and Geoff Benge.

- Geography books are grouped by area or topic. For

example, books about rivers are together, as are books about continents or states.

- Art and drawing books and supplies are all kept together. If a student wants to learn how to draw horses, the book that shows how to do this is on the same shelf as the coloring books, colored pencils, crayons, and paper.

- Music books, whether a book of musical compositions or the juvenile book about the history of American folk songs, are kept on the back of the piano or in the piano bench.

- One of my favorite sections is foreign language books, which include audio CDs, dictionaries, and flash cards. There are also books about word origins and the history of the English language.

- Reference books make up the final area. These include dictionaries, thesauruses, and oversized books used for reference.

I recommend that series books be kept together. That way children know exactly where to find the next book in a series if they've read one and enjoyed it.

In addition to the above areas, we also have general children's fiction books, which include picture books, storybooks, and board books. We keep these books low on the bookshelves so that even young children can have access to them throughout the day. I've been in homes with very few children's books, and the books that are available are high up on shelves where children can't reach them. Children will develop a greater appreciation for books if they have access to them and feel like the books are theirs to enjoy.

If you are just starting out with homeschooling and you only have a few books, I recommend that you organize as you go. Many families prefer to check books out of the library, and that's great! If you want to add to your own collection, however, plan ahead. If you already have a lot of books and there is no system for storing them, I encourage you to take a few days and organize them into categories like the ones I've suggested. It will only take a few hours, or days, depending on how many books you have, but the time you'll save later will be well worth the investment now! I can't imagine how difficult it would be to homeschool or what our home would look like if we didn't have our books organized.

DOWNSIZING

The average American household has an overabundance of material items. In the homeschooling household, when you add in all the books, pencils, papers, art supplies, workbooks, games, puzzles, and other educational products, it creates even more clutter. Since some educational materials are necessary for your homeschooling endeavors, you may have to make space to keep these materials by getting rid of things that have less meaning to you now.

We've already talked about how children can help with chores and the various ways you can organize cleaning tasks. We've also talked about removing clutter through seasonal cleaning. Another suggestion for dealing with clutter is to think about downsizing. This involves a lot more than your average daily or even seasonal cleaning. Basically there are three steps:

1. Go through old paperwork, magazines, newspapers, broken toys, etc., and throw away trash.
2. Sort things (outgrown clothes, toys no longer played with, extra dishes) that you no longer use. If they are still in usable condition, consider selling them, donating them to charity, or giving them to a friend who can use them.
3. Keep the things that are most precious to you, and since you will get rid of a lot of clutter in the previous two steps, use your newly cleaned space to organize what's left.

Of course, these three steps sound simple enough, but they are not, particularly if it involves going through a lot of clutter. The first time we tried to downsize, it took several months because we had about thirteen years' worth of stuff to sort through. Now I try to go through the house about every six months and remove excessive clutter.

I believe downsizing is one of the most helpful tools in organizing a home. There isn't enough space here to include the story that led our family to downsize and the subsequent blessings of it, but visit my Web site (*www .thehomeschooladvocate.com*) for that story, plus specific tips, advice, and suggestions for getting your family on board to help. Once you downsize the first time, it gets easier to do it again later, and it also makes daily and seasonal cleaning easier without all the extra clutter.

> I have a plaque by my front door that says, "My house was clean last week, sorry you missed it."
>
> —Michelle C., Pennsylvania

LIVING WITH THE STATUS QUO

I want to close this chapter with Ecclesiastes 3:1, which says, "There is a time for everything, and a season for every activity under heaven." If you are called to homeschool, this might be your season for a messy house while you focus on the educational needs of your child. And although it might not make it any easier to bear when no one has clean socks, try to remember the homeschooling mom down the street who seems to have it all together but who is probably also worried about her family having clean socks to wear!

Chapter 10

Dealing With Relatives

If you're fortunate, your relatives will see your children as blessings and agree with your basic parenting techniques. If you're truly fortunate, they'll support your decision to homeschool them!

Unfortunately, many of us go through a period where we either have to convince our relatives that homeschooling is the right choice or, at the very least, that it's our choice to make even if they don't agree with it.

With our relatives, we've had to learn techniques for maintaining a healthy relationship.

SET BOUNDARIES AND ESTABLISH RULES

Make it clear to your relatives that you respect them and love them, but that you must make the decisions about how to raise your child.

It might be good to share with your relatives the reasons why homeschooling is a good choice for your child.

Emphasize that while you respect their opinions, you do not

want them to discuss the issue of homeschooling (or any issue pertaining to your parenting or discipline) in front of your child.

If you are going to teach based on a schedule, it might be helpful to share this with your relatives. This serves a dual purpose. (1) They can see that you are taking your decision to homeschool seriously, and (2) you can ask them not to drop by unannounced during schooltime since this disrupts your lessons. If they would like to see your home school in action, invite them over for a day to visit.

Despite the request to share their opinions with you and not your child, if a relative repeatedly tells your child that he or she "should be in school" or should "ask to go to school," you may need to go with your spouse and talk with the individual together.

> I think the world is looking for us to fail. There are even many grandparents who wish us to fail so they can be "right" about our decision to homeschool. This is pressure that we should not have to worry about.
>
> —Elizabeth B., Kentucky

Let them know that this isn't acceptable and if they continue to do this, you'll have to be present when they visit your child. This may seem like an insignificant issue, but a discontented heart opens the door for sin. After all, it was discontent (or a desire for something different) that led to most sins throughout history, including original sin. The serpent sowed the seeds of discontent in Eve, who then shared this discontent with Adam, and they both ate the forbidden fruit. While public or private school certainly isn't "forbidden fruit," if the parents have decided that home school is the best option for the child, relatives should not be trying to convince the child otherwise.

If homeschooling is the only issue that causes friction in the relationship with your relatives, you are fortunate. When you're together, rather than focusing on homeschooling, try to keep the focus on common interests—sports, weather, genealogy, or other topics.

LAUGHING AT OURSELVES

The older I grow, the more I learn to laugh at myself. This has been very helpful with regard to relationships with our relatives. One day we invited Chris's parents to visit, and the night before they were supposed to arrive, we had a moms' get-together at our house. Unfortunately, during the evening, a chocolate fondue pot exploded in the dining room. That same night, my daughter left a bottle of ink on the dining room table and one of the cats knocked it over. While we slept, the cat proceeded to explore the dark, watery fluid that leaked through a crack in the table. When we awoke the next morning, in addition to finding more chocolate in places, there were little black paw prints all over our white dining room floor and across the living room carpet! And all this in time for the arrival of Chris's dad and stepmom!

Over the years, we've had many such accidents or incidents occur in our home! I've learned to accept my imperfections, laugh at myself, and turn these times into fun memories. Find the common ground with your relatives. Even if you don't get along well with them, set your boundaries and stick to them. Then be willing to laugh at yourself and try not to justify your actions.

> Most of my aunts and uncles homeschooled their kids, and my mom and dad did so with their last two so they know it from both angles. My in-laws are supportive although they have no experience with it, but they really like how we're raising our kids so far.
>
> —Laura M., Canada

> My mum has always been supportive. My mum-in-law has always been against our homeschooling. Even after six years she hasn't "come round," although I think she is finally softening to the idea.
>
> —Lara K., New Zealand

PRAY

I can't tell you how many homeschooling parents have said that their relatives were initially opposed to the concept of homeschooling, but they've come around over time. Many of their relatives are now wholeheartedly supportive of the decision!

I just knew the decision we had made was right, so I tried patiently to answer the questions as they came up, and peacefully rejected criticism. There was a lot of it. Now they see the multiple interests and talents of my children that are not usually developed in their public-schooled peers, and they often compliment our decision and how incredible our kids are. They also notice the wonderful relationships we have in our family and compare their public-schooled peers and lament that many of them have little or no relationship with their siblings and are often even lacking in relationship with their parents. It has taken time, so we had to be patient and keep praying that God would change their hearts, but I can honestly say after almost six years, I can't think of a single relative who is against our homeschooling! And that is a miracle!

—Casey M., missionary home-schooler in the Philippines

God can work miracles in people's hearts. Remember to take this issue before the Lord in prayer.

Meanwhile, invite your relatives to home-school events—recitals, ball games, or grand-parent nights at your co-op. It's not necessary to show them your child's schoolwork, but you can leave subtle reminders that your child is learn-ing. Allow them to see your child reading books, pursuing a talent, or playing with other children (since one of the biggest concerns of relatives is whether or not they will be socialized). If your child receives excellent scores on standardized achievement tests, you might share these with relatives.

Chapter 11

Homeschooling on a Budget

While "perfect" homeschooling families have always had a plan, paid off all their debt before they had children, and never seem to have any financial woes, the average homeschooling family (that is, the majority of us) typically makes ends meet through supplemental income of some sort, struggles to balance their checkbook from month to month, and frequently worries about unexpected expenses because there is no cash reserve. Many homeschooling families participate in debt-reduction programs, such as Dave Ramsey's Financial Peace University. Even as they try to reduce their debt, families are struggling in an economy where expenses have increased and income has decreased. In this chapter, you'll find some practical suggestions for saving money, decreasing your debt, and making extra money at home.

Now, I'm not a financial counselor, but theoretically, financial peace should be attainable if a person is willing to spend less and pay off debt. I say "theoretically" because I know we cannot be the only family who has faithfully followed the suggestions in the financial programs, yet we continue to have debt. Before Chris and I were married, we took on a small amount of debt to purchase a vehicle. When we were married, we added to this debt to pay for our honeymoon. We shouldn't have done that perhaps, but we didn't have a lot of debt and we had it paid off within a year. Sarah was born about two years later, and at that time we were debt free but we had no savings. This was a huge mistake. We purchased our first home while I was pregnant with Sarah, and I quit my job soon after she was born. We could no longer make the house payment with one income, so a year to the day after we purchased the house, we sold it at a loss. We had built up some debt during that year because we had to pay for food and bills with credit cards. Even though our living situation was much cheaper after we sold the house, Micah was born less than a year later and he had a lot of health problems, and thus medical bills. We had more debt than ever.

We worked diligently over the next few years, and by the time Hannah came along, we were happily debt free again. We still had no savings, however, and we lived paycheck to paycheck with no financial breathing room. During the next year, doctors' offices continually threatened to turn us over to collection agencies because we owed so much. Finally I buckled under the stress and put all the bills on credit cards. It was a great relief that they weren't calling me anymore, but it was a huge financial mistake. Six years later, we are still paying off these medical bills with the added burden of interest.

I've had all sorts of advice concerning our finances. Some people said we never should have put the medical bills on interest-bearing credit cards, but they weren't living with the stress of badgering phone calls, and besides, that advice doesn't do a lot of good when it's given after the fact! I was so sick at the time, I just wanted peace. One well-meaning person told us that we had debt because we weren't tithing a full 10 percent every single week. Others told me that I should have sued the hospital for the horrible ways they botched my care and caused permanent damage. I agree with that one!

Sometimes families will tell me that they are conscientious about their spending, live frugally, put all extra money toward debt, don't use—or stopped using—credit cards, but they simply cannot make ends meet. I sympathize with these families. If you are in this situation, I honestly do understand. Although we are not yet debt free, I have some practical suggestions that have kept us afloat, and I hope they'll offer you some relief as well. Maybe you'll even be fortunate enough to do better than stay afloat!

> Having had my kids in school for a few years before I started homeschooling, I definitely think homeschooling puts a LOT more stress on the mother. Not only does she have to adapt to having her kids around her 24/7, but she also has to learn the whole "homeschooling thing" and cope with the new financial pressure, and her husband has to cope with less attention from his wife (at first at least).
>
> —Wendy H., New Zealand

FINDING FREE ITEMS

One of the best ways to save money is simply to avoid spending money. This is actually easier than people think, but lots of people neglect to put this into practice until it's too late. There are many things people can do without and we'll address that later in this chapter, but for now we're going to start with finding free items and work up to earning extra income at home.

Several years ago I was taking something to the thrift store and I thought about how many other homeschooling families might be able to use the items in my van. I wasn't sure how to get the items to the families and I certainly didn't want to keep them in my house while I was trying to clean and get rid of stuff. Finally, the idea came to start a Swap Day.

Within a few days, it was scheduled. We encouraged families to gather up things they were no longer using and bring them to our co-op on the scheduled date. Everyone was welcome to look through the items and take what they wanted, whether they brought something or not. Since the goal was to help people get rid of unused items and clutter in their homes and bless others who couldn't afford to purchase the items, it didn't really matter who brought what.

I've seen similar events sponsored at homeschool co-ops and even churches across the country. If your co-op is not already doing this, it's a terrific ministry. You'll help families clean out clutter and you'll bless families by providing them with clothing and other items they need but cannot afford. Since we allowed people to bring anything to the swap, people would frequently leave with schoolbooks, furniture, clothing, even boxes or cans of food that someone decided they didn't want or need.

There are three general ways to handle clean-up: (1) The organizer gathers up everything that's left and takes it to the thrift store. (2) Some nonprofit organizations will pick up leftovers if arranged in advance. (3) Require that everyone who brought items take them back and do with them as they wish.

If you do not participate in a co-op, I would encourage you to arrange a Swap Day through a local church or community organization. If your children are still very young, you might contact a local MOPS group about hosting a swap there. If you have teens, find out if the youth group might be interested in sponsoring a Swap Day.

Another resource available in most communities is Freecycle. According to *www.freecycle.org,* there are Freecycle groups across the globe. The groups are made up of people who want to keep good stuff out of landfills by getting things into the hands of someone who can use it. Members of the group post what they have to give away and take what they can use. Visit the Web site to see if there is one in your community. We've picked up tomato plants, books, and a humidifier on Freecycle, and we've given away tons of stuff.

In addition to Freecycle, you might also be able to find free items in your local newspaper or through a local homeschool e-mail loop. If there isn't a homeschool e-mail loop in your area, these are easy to start!

Finally, if you need something and you are trying to save money, don't forget to check the dump. When we take our trash to the trash/recycle center, we have no intention of taking anything away, but occasionally there is something too nice to pass up. One day we found fifteen beautiful folding metal chairs in the trash! Since we frequently host large homeschool parties at our home, this was a wonderful find!

We live in a rural area so we're expected to take our excess garbage to the trash center. Some people don't want to do this so they'll put perfectly good items on the side of the road for others to pick up. We always ask just in case, and we've found a Little Tykes easel, several brand-new rolls of Christmas paper and boxes of ornaments, and some beautiful dishes. It still amazes me what people throw away!

Whether you're sponsoring a Swap Day, participating in Freecycle, making use of someone else's trash, or simply accepting hand-me-downs, finding free items is one of the best ways to save money. If anyone makes negative comments about your creativity, remind them that we already have too much stuff in the world so you are not only helping your family financially, but you are also preserving the environment!

BARTERING

When finding something free isn't possible, you might consider bartering for the products or services you can't live without.

Bartering basically means that you exchange another person's products or services for your own products or services. People have been doing this for centuries, and I'm certain this form of exchange will take place long into the future.

Here is a sample of things you can barter:

- Material goods/products (clothing, books, toys, furniture, appliances)
- Haircuts
- Tutoring
- Lawn care
- Computer repair
- Painting
- Plumbing
- Chimney work
- Dental care
- Nail care
- Food/meal preparation
- Massage therapy
- Tax preparation
- Baby-sitting
- Photography
- Chiropractic care
- Use of time share/vacation home
- Lessons—piano, art, flight instruction, driving
- Pet sitting
- Housecleaning
- Automotive repair

Look for barter opportunities. If you grow a garden and your green peppers are more prolific than you expected, ask someone at the local farmer's market if they would be willing to trade green peppers for something you need, such as strawberries. It's a great way to save money!

SAVING MONEY ON BOOKS AND CURRICULUM

One expense that almost all homeschoolers have in common is books and curriculum. If you are homeschooling, you already know the amount of money that can be spent on books in a year. If you are not yet homeschooling, this is something you will need to be prepared for. Here are some suggestions to help you save money on homeschool supplies.

1. Set a homeschool supply budget for the year and stick to it. Don't forget to set aside a monthly amount that you can use for items continually purchased throughout the year.
2. Buy used on the Internet. Don't get caught up in bidding frenzies and pay more than the material is worth! Compare prices to those on the publisher's Web site. Also be sure to visit *www.vegsource.com* and *www.homeschoolclassifieds.com* for used materials.
3. Make use of the local library. Before you purchase anything, see if you can find the books you need at the library or through an interlibrary loan. Also, let them know which items you would like to see on the shelves; it helps determine their purchases.
4. Trade books and curriculum from one year to the next with another family who is using the same curriculum at different grade levels.
5. Share materials with another family during the same school year. You can do this with items like science supplies, reading books, or sports equipment. You could even plan to use the items together, such as getting together once a week to do science experiments and participate in sports.

6. Take advantage of free materials available on the Internet—online educational games, printable work sheets, and so on. There are also some wonderful educational videos and audio materials available for download.

7. Ask people for their old magazines. Most of the time when people have finished with their most recent copy of a magazine, they are willing to share it. Make sure you approve of the content.

8. When possible, buy materials that can be passed down to younger children.

9. If you have more than one child, buy science, history, art, music, and Bible curriculum that you can use with different ages at the same time.

10. Attend library book sales. You can find wonderful deals through your local library sales, and many times they have books available for purchase throughout the year.

11. Find out if anyone else in your area sponsors used book sales. Sometimes nonprofit groups, hospitals, or even private schools will sponsor used book sales.

12. Attend used-curriculum sales sponsored by local or regional homeschool groups. Some sales also allow desks, bookshelves, educational toys, puzzles, and games.

13. You can also find some terrific deals on books, especially older books, at thrift stores, garage sales, flea markets, and used bookstores.

14. If you prefer new homeschool curriculum or if you are registered through a satellite school that requires new curriculum, purchase this at a curriculum fair, where you're likely to receive a discount directly from the publisher and also save money on shipping.

15. Take care of your books so that they can be re-sold more easily.

16. If you aren't sure which homeschool curriculum or method you want to use, ask friends if you can borrow their materials for a week or two until you decide what is right for your family. If

that's not possible, see if you can get sample pages online, or find older, worn-out copies of books that are no longer saleable.

17. Unless there is a reason why you need a newer edition, purchase older versions. Newer editions almost always cost more.

18. Make sure you need the teacher materials before you purchase them. Frequently you can easily teach without teacher materials, especially for the lower-grade subjects.

19. Sell your used materials. In addition to books and curriculum, don't forget to take good care of flash cards, manipulatives (objects used in teaching to reinforce a lesson), teacher materials, and other supplies related to home school that you might be able to resell.

20. If you purchase directly from a publisher, try to combine your order with that of homeschool friends. You will most likely save money on shipping, plus you might qualify for a quantity discount.

21. If you're willing to use them, ask for old school texts. I personally think these books are dull and boring, but you can find some good things among the materials, such as maps, transparencies, and work sheets.

CUTTING HOUSEHOLD EXPENSES

I've read stories about moms who have cut their grocery bill in half by using coupons and changing their shopping habits. Since many homeschooling families have three or more children, the monthly grocery bill can easily be close to $1,000 or more. We use the following techniques to keep our spending on grocery and household items within a reasonable range.

- Stockpile sale items. To save money, buy items when they are on sale. Don't forget to stock up on nonperishable items such as toilet paper, aluminum foil, light bulbs, and paper towels as well.

- Compare quantity price. Sometimes it doesn't save money to buy in bulk, so check to see which items have the best deal per ounce.

- Plan ahead. Browse circulars and newspapers for specials. Make note of the best deals to stockpile. Jonni McCoy, of *www.miserlymoms.com,* recommends that you purchase items from the front and back of the flier, because that's where the best deals are, and plan your weekly meals around those sale items. McCoy was able to cut her grocery bill in half when she began using this and other shopping tricks. Also, to cut down on hunger-induced impulse buys, don't forget to eat before you go, and give your children a snack before you head to the store.

- Watch for specials. Take advantage of double coupons, frequent-shopper discounts, and in-store specials. While the store bonus programs can be complex, they usually save you money.

- Participate in store "clubs." Grocery store chains are starting to give customers the option to sign up for a Baby Club, Kids Club, Pet Club, and the like. Why not sign up and enjoy the savings?

- Make your own products. Many homeschoolers sew their own clothing, make their own laundry detergent, grow their own vegetables, and bake their own bread, among other things. As I said in the first chapter, the purpose of this book is not to make you feel guilty or incompetent, so if you don't do these things or have no desire to do them, that's okay! However, for families who want another way to cut costs, see if you can make it, bake it, or grow it more economically on your own.

- Cook ahead. When you purchase sale items in bulk, cook an extra meal from the ingredients and put it in the freezer. When you don't have time to cook a full meal, you can use one of your homemade frozen dinners and avoid eating out, which can be costly.

In chapter 9, I talked about downsizing from the perspective of getting rid of clutter and cleaning your home. When you downsize, however, don't forget to take advantage of the massive amount of stuff that you'll be taking out of your house. Sell these things and use the money to pay off debt. Once you've sold, donated, or given away the extra clutter you were holding on to, you might actually be able to live in a smaller home. After we downsized, we moved our family of seven from a 3,000-square-foot home to a 1,500-square-foot home. Now, I'll admit that at times it's a bit cramped, but we love our home and everyone understands the concept of sharing.

CUTTING OTHER EXPENSES

When we were downsizing, we not only sold about half of our belongings but we also evaluated ways to cut other expenses. This is easier than people think, but you have to be willing to make sacrifices, small and large.

Here are some things a family may cut from its budget:

- Extra phone services, such as caller ID and voicemail
- Cell phone service
- Cable service
- Satellite service
- Entertainment expenses
- Eating out expenses
- Professional/salon haircuts
- Manicure and pedicure expenses
- Lawn maintenance expenses

Only you can decide which things are necessities for your family. Taking into consideration my health issues, the fact that we travel frequently, and the fact that we have young children, we decided that home and cell phone service was a necessity, not a frivolous expense.

When we moved, we eliminated cable television. Now we subscribe to Netflix, an Internet-based movie rental program. This has turned out to be a very good investment for us since we rent educational movies, documentaries, children's shows, and other things that we want to watch for one low monthly fee. We can also watch movies through their instant-download option. This is less than $20 per month—much cheaper than cable or satellite—and there is no temptation to keep the television on.

The world is also full of free entertainment:

- Take a walk with your children.
- Play a board game with the family.
- Go to the park.
- Go outside and play ball or Frisbee.
- Tell stories or read a book out loud.
- Listen to a book on audiotape.
- Make cookies with your children.
- Spend the afternoon doing science experiments.
- Ride bikes.
- Develop a new hobby.
- Play music with your family.

If you are compelled to go out for entertainment, limit this to special occasions and look for the best deals. For our family of seven, it would cost $56 just for tickets to see an evening movie. Matinees are cheaper, but we still avoid the theater. Be willing to change your habits for the sake of your budget. Downsizing is not only reducing the clutter in your life and paying off debt, but it also means changing your lifestyle to cut any unnecessary expenses.

Eating out has been the most difficult expense for us to eliminate. My health problems make it difficult for me to be on my feet for very long and also to digest the food I eat. However, I have found ways to eat out that are compatible with our budget. Some restaurants don't mind if adults order from the children's menu. These meals can be as much as 75 percent cheaper than adult meals and the smaller portion size is preferential for some people.

MEDICAL BILLS

Sometimes financial woes are related to circumstances beyond our control. When you are dealing with ongoing illness, disabilities, or other health issues, you will most likely have bills that increase your stress even more. Here are some ideas that might help you cope with medical bills:

- When you have medical procedures, try to find out up front what the cost of the procedure will be and try to negotiate a lower fee. This is becoming more difficult to do since many fees are set in stone, but ask anyway. You might be pleasantly surprised.

- For medical bills that you can plan for in advance, find out if you can make payments on the bill in advance.

- Find out if paying a bill in full within a certain period makes you eligible for a reduction.

- Ask your doctor for samples of a new medication before you pay a co-pay to purchase it at the pharmacy. We've wasted a lot of money buying medicine that we ended up not being able to use because the person was allergic to it or had severe side effects.

- When you're financially strapped, ask for samples of regular medications.

- Ask your doctor if a medicine is absolutely necessary for you to take or if you can do without it.

- Many prescription medications are now available over the counter at a lower cost, so ask first.

- Find out if you can see a nurse practitioner. They are highly qualified, and seeing one may lower your visit fee.

- If you simply need lab work or a shot, ask if you can schedule an appointment with a nurse rather than an office visit with the doctor. This can make the difference between a $120 bill and a $20 bill.

EARN MONEY WORKING AT HOME

If you've reduced expenses and you still have a lot of debt to pay off or you're having difficulty meeting your monthly expenses, you may need to increase your income. One of the most obvious ways to do this is to start a home business.

There are several things to take into account when considering which home business would be appropriate for you:

- your natural talents and abilities

- your computer skills

- how much time you are able to devote to a home business

- hours, days, or weeks that you are available to work
- transportation issues
- what services/products are needed in your area
- the space you have available to devote to a home business (office space, product storage)

Frequently people are unaware of their options. Below is a list of businesses I would recommend for homeschooling moms. You will need to take into account the requirements for each business and match it up to the above list with your own desires, abilities, resources, and time restraints.

As a new business-woman and long-time homeschooler, often I would rather be working instead of schooling. I have to constantly evaluate what I am doing with my children. . . . Did I spend enough time with them today? Did they have a teacher when they needed one? Or did I brush them off because I was busy answering customer e-mails. It's very important that I hold myself accountable to my most important clients: my children—my students.

—Amy O., New Jersey

- deliver newspapers, magazines, fliers, or coupon books
- write freelance articles for newspapers, magazines, or Web sites
- provide child care for a working mom
- sell something through home shows (Avon, Mary Kay, Tupperware)
- open an online store and sell books, toys, jewelry, or other items. (It's easy to open these stores through eBay, and lots of homeschool moms are doing this.)
- offer typing services for college students
- do transcription or billing for a doctor's office
- sell food from your garden or orchard
- raise and sell animals (rabbits, guinea pigs, chickens, goats, mice)

- offer computer repair
- cook meals for working moms

Keep your priorities in mind if you're going to run a home business. It's easy for moms with perfectionist tendencies to also have an inclination toward compulsiveness. With this combination, it can be tempting to become a workaholic, especially when homeschooling becomes frustrating. If you face these issues, it might be helpful to keep priorities in order, reevaluate your need to work at home on a regular basis, and continue to focus on the reasons you decided to homeschool in the first place.

REMEMBER DAD

While I was doing research and conducting interviews for this book, I asked dads what their biggest source of stress was. The highest percentage of homeschool dads said financial pressure. Other sources of stress for dads were worrying about whether the children were receiving an adequate education and worrying about the health of the homeschooling mom. While many recognized their responsibilities as the spiritual head of the home, most of the dads said that they saw their biggest responsibility as that of breadwinner and protector of his bride.

It was really neat to be able to read hundreds of interviews and see the dedication most of these homeschool dads feel for the homeschool moms. Hopefully there will be some dads reading this book who will find the comments about fathers encouraging. Also, I mention this here to remind moms that just as our heavenly Father cares for us, an earthly father feels an extreme amount of pressure to be a good provider for his family. He might express his concerns differently, but stress can be just as overwhelming for dads as it is for moms. Encourage your husband often.

Chapter 12

The Special Needs Child at Home

Families who have a child with special needs aren't exempt from the pressure to be perfect. In many ways, these families probably feel more stress than other homeschoolers. They have attention drawn to their family not only because they homeschool but also because they are trying to teach a child with special needs.

We live in a society that has been trained to think that children, especially children with special needs, are best served in settings where trained professionals can teach them what they need to know. Because of this, homeschooling families face an uphill battle. When a parent of a special needs child wants to homeschool, they frequently need to dig in their heels and be ready for a battle. This isn't always the case, but you'll need to be ready. Perhaps you've already been through the battle!

With modern technology, many parents find out their child has a health problem before the child is even born. In other cases, they knowingly adopt a child with special needs. Every situation will be unique and every child has challenges. If your child has particular physical, mental, or emotional needs, it does not necessarily mean a professional can do a better job teaching your child. If anything, these children need their parents more than ever, so I applaud your decision to teach them at home. It is my prayer that you'll find the following information useful as you begin, or continue, your journey.

SUPPORT GROUPS

There are many terrific support groups for families who have a child with special needs. Find out what resources they offer and join the one that best fits your unique needs as a family. There are general support groups and there are support groups related to a child's specific challenge. You'll find these locally and nationally. Don't forget to consider Web-based support groups, as these can provide helpful articles, encouragement, and ideas.

One group specifically for homeschoolers who have a child with special needs is National Challenged Homeschoolers Associated Network (NATHHAN). You can find out more about this terrific support group at *www.nathhan.org*.

DEALING WITH THE PUBLIC SCHOOL SYSTEM

If your child has never been in the public school system and you have a supportive pediatrician, you may not encounter much pressure to put your child in school. However, if your doctor insists on a public education for your special needs child so that he will have access to certain services, try to explain that you believe home-schooling would be best for your child. If he still pushes for public school, you should be polite and listen to his views, but after the visit, you may want to consider finding a homeschool-friendly pediatrician.

Once your child has been in public school or if you have

somehow become involved with someone from the school system (previous use of special services, for example, or a doctor's referral), then you may have to deal with a little more opposition.

In situations where someone is pushing you to put your child in the public school system, be ready to defend your position. Whether your child has special needs or not, he is still your child, and parents should be allowed to decide what is best for their child.

If you aren't already aware of this, public schools receive a particular amount of funding for every child who enrolls. When they classify a child with special needs, the school system receives a greater allotment of money. I believe this is one reason why there has been a greater number of children "diagnosed" with various learning problems within the school setting. The school system knows that once they diagnose that child, the diagnosis typically follows him or her, and the school will continue to receive more money throughout that child's education years. In my opinion, this is also why public schools want those homeschooled children with special needs. They would receive more funding if the parents put them in public school. (If

We have one son, Luke-John. He was adopted when he was two-and-a-half years old. He was very malnourished, frightened, and insecure when he came to live with us. At the age of six, we realized that Luke-John was not like other children in the sense that he could not master reading, writing, and math as quickly as others. . . . Luke-John decided of his own accord to leave school in the middle of August 2008 (grade 4). At the time, he was severely depressed and anxious. He continually complained of stomachaches and headaches. Furthermore, he was being ridiculed in class because of his inabilities. The teacher did not do much to stop the ridicule, even though we had spoken to her on more than one occasion. We allowed Luke-John to have a month off, just to get used to the idea of being at home. At the beginning of October, we started homeschooling. I took him back into grade 1, starting with the absolute basics. Right through October and November we worked through various books, helping him to understand. I quickly realized that there was nothing the matter with my child other than learning in a different way. Luke-John has returned to being a normal twelve-year-old boy. He too is happy that he is being homeschooled. His confidence is slowly returning and he is catching up to where he is supposed to be at an astronomical rate. If I could turn back the clock, I would have started homeschooling much sooner and not put Luke-John through the trauma he went through.

—Gary and Sandy L., South Africa

you encounter someone who says that homeschoolers are "taking" money from the public school system, it's important to remember that the money allotted to the school system is intended for the care and education of a student. If a student is receiving care and education at home, then the public school system isn't spending any money on him and therefore doesn't need that funding.)

EDUCATION-RELATED LAWS

The Individuals with Disabilities Education Improvement Act (IDEA) is a federal law that requires states to provide a free and appropriate public education for each eligible child with a disability. Notice that this says "public" education. For children in alternative educational environments, such as private schools or home schools, the law is different.

In the case of children who do not attend public school, the local education agency is required to spend a proportionate amount of money serving these children, but the amount of money and the services available are nowhere near what the children in public schools receive. Additionally, if you happen to live in a county like mine, where the local education agency has been traditionally biased against homeschoolers, you may find that all the extra funding goes toward helping children in private schools but not homeschoolers. Since the law doesn't specify how to distribute the money, other than the fact that it must be made available to students in alternative school settings, it's very easy to deny homeschoolers access to these services.

For the fortunate parents who live in a county where the local education agency is not biased, you may find that your local system is more than willing to help you discover your child's problems, suggest appropriate treatments or therapies, and even provide some of those services.

In general, become familiar with the education-related laws

where you live. For example, are you required to register your home school? Do you have to submit a portfolio? Is the local education agency asking for paperwork that is not legally required?

SET GOALS

Every child is different, but even with the vast array of special needs children can have, these children also have a large variety of abilities. Some children need someone to feed them, while others simply need help walking. In every homeschool setting, it's good to set goals, because goals help you remember where you were headed if you get sidetracked. In a special needs household, goals are particularly helpful so that you can not only remember where you were headed but also so that you can look back over the weeks, months, and years at the progress your child has made!

When you set goals for your child, remember to set goals that are challenging yet attainable. Does the child have the physical or mental capability to achieve the goals you've set? Is your child emotionally ready to tackle new challenges? Don't fall into the perfectionist trap of trying to "look good" for others! Forget about the rest of the world for a moment, look at your child, and set those goals based on your child's needs and abilities.

MAKING THE MOST OF OUTSIDE ACTIVITIES

As you undoubtedly know, good preparation often makes the difference in successful outings with children who have special needs. For example, if you have a child with sensory issues and suddenly someone turns on blaring music, it's going to startle the child. It can sometimes take hours to settle him down, so it's best to prepare him—or the environment—in advance. When you decide to take

> [Our son] has Asperger's syndrome, so the school setting wasn't the best environment for him. After reading and working with him for a little while, God started to work in my heart, calling me to homeschool my girls too. I realized that the safest place to learn was our home. My kids were ready and I was willing.
>
> —Claudine A., British Columbia

your child on outings, field trips, or to birthday parties, you may want to take the following into consideration:

- temperature, weather conditions
- noise level
- distracting smells (my son used to get sick at church because of women's perfume)
- bright lights
- crowds
- dangerous objects, sharp corners, breakable items
- exposure to germs
- exposure to allergens

Whether you want to take your child on outings or enroll her in a co-op class, you can also take steps to help prepare your child for participation in outside activities. Here are some suggestions:

- Talk with your child about the setting in advance.
- Train your child to sit still.
- Practice at home (e.g., pretend you're at church and expose your child to the music and other activities so that he will know what to expect).
- Gradually introduce your child to new settings and people.
- Prepare others for potential disruption as well. Let others (co-op teachers, leaders, etc.) know in advance that your child may require special services or attention.

When you participate in outside activities, let others know that you may need to leave early. Your child is your priority. All children can be manipulative, so make sure he is genuinely stressed with a situation, then leave and try again later.

EMPHASIZE LIFE SKILLS

Of course abilities will vary for each child, but one of the best things parents of children with special needs can do is integrate life skills training into their homeschool setting. Actually, I believe this is one of the reasons children with special needs do so well learning at home! Homeschooling parents are able to emphasize independence, life skills, and even work skills.

It might be helpful to make a list of life skills you want your child to learn. Determine which things your child can already do and then decide which things you will help your child learn each year. In addition to the life skills listed in chapter 7, you may want to integrate the following into your child's educational portfolio:

- memorization of personal information, such as full name, address, telephone number

- money skills (identification of coins, value of coins and paper money, how to make change)

- how to read a clock and tell time, preferably with both digital and analog clocks

- basic understanding of daily routines (waking up, getting dressed, eating meals, going to bed)

- basic literacy skills

- how to read social signals, such as identifying when someone is angry

- community signs such as pedestrian crossings, wet walking

> We have three children with special needs. We've learned how to best deal with these obstacles by educating ourselves and then tweaking the education to fit our particular needs. This was extremely difficult, but so worth the effort when you see the light bulb come on in their brain; attitudes change and a new life opens up in front of them! ... The person who knows your child best is YOU, the PARENT! I hate it when people think that if someone has a few extra letters after their name, they know what's best for everyone. The letters behind my name are MOM, and I will listen and glean info from the professionals, but I will listen to my gut instinct every time.
> —Janice H., Tennessee

Our youngest has had differences in his manners for years, but we attributed them to who he was—an original, like all the other kids. Reading, like for the other boys, was a challenge. Phonics and sight words were repeated and repeated. Math came easy, and so life went. Then a grand mal seizure; later, night terrors, more seizures . . . and slowly the rose-colored glasses came off. Our son did not have a reading struggle alone, but there were several things that were not quite on par with "typical" kids his age. Now at eleven years of age we have begun to connect the dots and are soon to test for a name for the chain of things that has been part of the fabric of his life. We have taken Sam as he came to us, calling his way of living life "Sam time." We sometimes slow down to catch up to him, other times he pushes himself harder to catch up to us. It has been a dance and an obstacle course; not really sure where the end will take us or where we really are going.

—Mary V., Alabama

area, exit signs, stop signs, no smoking, no parking, and out-of-order signs

• important labels such as poison, flammable, high voltage, prescription medicines

• how to read recipes, directions, maps, calendars

• familiarity with different types of community buildings and their services (grocery store, bank, post office, Laundromat, hardware store, beauty/barber shop, pharmacy)

• rules about not touching or how to use appliances, such as stove, toaster, microwave, blender

• how to complete a job application

ACCEPTANCE

Finally, accept your child for who he or she is. God does not make mistakes. We live in a sinful world where health problems and the degeneration of our bodies have made us increasingly more susceptible to illness, disease, and disorders, but life itself is never an error.

While the members of every family should rally around one another, love one another, and accept one another for who each is, many parents still succumb to worldly expectations and try to "fix" a child. We should always strive to help every child reach his or her full potential, but it's also important to recognize that some children may have limitations. These limitations do not have to define the child; rather, focus can be placed on the abilities the child possesses.

Chapter 13

Following Your Own Path

When we have gone hiking with the children, we check the maps at the base of the trails to study the different routes and decide which one is best for our family. Some trails are relatively straight but might require extensive climbing. Other trails are long and winding, providing views along the way, but take a lot longer to reach the destination. Since we have young children, we usually take the long, winding trails that tend to be safer—without dangerous overhangs, lots of dense foliage to tread through, or excessive climbing. The children love these long, winding paths because they get to look at small critters, pick up fallen leaves, discover mushrooms or other plants, and enjoy time with Mom and Dad. I must say, though, that by the time I reach the end of the long, winding path, it sometimes feels like I'm going to die!

No matter what the situation, it can be exhausting doing what you know is right and good for your child. There are times when I think I cannot handle another day of homeschooling. *I can't do it anymore!* I think. I just want to hurry up and drag the children with me past the dangerous overhangs, through the dense foliage, and up the cliffs of life, but I know that isn't the best path for them.

In reality, there is enough temptation and danger in life without purposefully subjecting ourselves to more. When we stand before the mountain of life, there are many paths to follow. I'm not talking about the straight and narrow path to the Lord Jesus. Rather, I'm referring to the many other choices we're given about how to live our lives. Some paths include marriage. Others include missionary work. Other paths include homeschooling.

THE BIBLE AS AN ACADEMIC RESOURCE

If you are not a Christian, it is my desire that something in these pages might open the door for you to desire a relationship with Christ. Perhaps you have decided to read a Bible that has been packed away in storage for years, or maybe you want to renew the relationship you once had with the Lord.

Whatever the circumstances, it may take time for your family to adjust to this concept. If your children are older, it might be more difficult. Of course, prayer is your first weapon of defense against attacks from those who might deter you as you seek the Lord. It can also be helpful to make contact with godly individuals, develop Christ-centered relationships, and worship with fellow believers.

From a practical standpoint, it might also be helpful to integrate the Bible into your daily curriculum. It is a life-changing book that covers a variety of subjects:

- The Bible gives us commandments that help us live peaceably with one another and with God (preschool counting: 1-10, law).

- It also gives us a history of mankind with specific genealogies (history, timelines).

- It talks about a worldwide flood, which is the source of our world's great coal and oil deposits and is most likely what ushered in the Ice Age (science).

- The Bible has weights and measurements (math), parables (storytelling, drama), and proverbs (discernment, wisdom).

Finally, the most important thing to remember is that the Bible helps us to see the big picture—from the beginning to the end—and to see our place in it. This is not only important with regard to academics, but all areas of life. After all, the Bible is the written account of how God created us and loved us so much that he gave us the freedom to choose. When we chose sin over an unblemished relationship with the Father, then he loved us enough to send his only Son to die on the cross for our sins. It is through his Son that we can have a relationship with the Father again (John 14:6–7).

PRACTICING WHAT WE PREACH

A good quotation to post somewhere it can be read again and again is: "We may talk but never teach, until we practice what we preach" (source unknown).

The struggle to be perfect in our homeschool household is probably an understatement of how I tried to make our home school in the beginning. I wanted to be like all the homeschooling families you see where everyone in the family gets along and the kids are always perfect. That didn't last long when I realized that is not my family. We are not perfect, and trying to be perfect made us all miserable. Our house is not always spotless and the children do not always get along perfectly. We also definitely have our bad days! After I realized that, we changed our goals to fit our family.

—Judy W., Tennessee

Homeschooling is a way of life. Academics, lessons, activities, and sports are an integral part of homeschooling, but when you teach your child at home, it becomes an integral part of your lifestyle. For those who use a structured curriculum, learning is a priority that defines other aspects of the family lifestyle, such as whether or not to follow a strict schedule. It doesn't matter how you homeschool, but once you make the decision it becomes your way of life.

This doesn't mean that you will always homeschool, nor is it a value statement about homeschooling versus other forms of education. What it does mean is that little eyes are frequently watching you. When you teach your child at home, it's difficult to hide your own weaknesses from them, and you certainly see those of your child. It's important to be honest with your child, be willing to admit when you're wrong, and practice emulating good behavior. Hopefully your child will see you practice what you preach and also respect what you teach.

CONTAGIOUS ATTITUDES

I don't like to be around negative people. They stress me out. Unfortunately, there have been times when I've had no choice, and the whole time I'm around the person, I feel my own attitude turning increasingly sour. Just like it's easier to teach when you practice what you preach, it's also easier to teach when those around you have a positive attitude, because attitudes are contagious!

> Remember to laugh together. The homeschooling years will be over too fast.
> —Mari S., New Zealand

> There are always uncertainties. You will doubt your abilities, and your children will not change into angels once you bring them home. But prayer has and will always give peace and patience. Always keep in mind why you started homeschooling. Check whether you still feel the same need.
> —Marelize K., South Africa

Have you ever seen an infectious-disease chart? It tracks the amazing spread of illness, often starting with a single individual. First one person is sick, and that person comes into contact with and infects ten others, then those ten infect ten others, and suddenly you have one hundred people who are sick within a matter of days. The same is true of negative attitudes.

In the homeschool environment, negative attitudes can affect your ability to teach your child, enforce boundaries and rules, and implement chores. Regardless of who is the source—you, your child, your spouse, another adult living in the home, regular visitors to your home, the television, the computer—it's encouraging to remember that just as negative attitudes are contagious, so are positive ones. Try to keep a positive attitude and allow your child to "catch" it!

> A cheerful heart is good medicine, but a crushed spirit dries up the bones. —Proverbs 17:22

SIFTING THROUGH ADVICE

As you make decisions about which trails to take, you'll need to sift through a *lot* of advice. Once you announce to the world that you're planning to homeschool, you'll have advice running out your ears! Of course, you can find advice on your own through the Internet, books, and magazine articles. When other homeschoolers find out that you're homeschooling, they'll share all sorts of advice with you. Relatives and friends are sure to share their advice. And ironically, even complete strangers will tell you what they think about homeschooling, how you should do it, or what you should do differently.

> Our homeschooling years have been a long adventure where I have grown and learned as much as my children. These years together have been so precious, certainly not perfect, but very real! The culmination of this experience for my children has created happy, confident, well-adjusted, meaningful contributors to our community.
> —Jennie F., Western Australia

The challenge will be sifting through the advice to find what works for your family. This applies to discipline techniques, curriculum, which support group to join, the best homeschool field trips, and so on. Here are some suggestions to keep you from being overwhelmed with all the advice and the numerous choices it brings.

First, listen to the advice of others. They might make a comment that will help you mend a strained relationship, choose a curriculum well-suited for your family, or find a homeschool gymnastics class.

Next, diligently examine your options. Sift through all the advice you've received and decide whether it's something you want

My children will set their own goals for now and in the future. As parents, we want them to see a glimpse of heaven in our home, the warmth of the heavenly Father in our love, and the joy in the sacrifice Christ made for us. We want them to feel empowered to do what is right. We want them to shine and be fully engaged in all they do and pursue. There is a wealth of knowledge and experiences out there and we want our children to search for these nuggets and find them. We want their character to grow from the selfish nature they were born with to a character that prompts them to consider the implications of their actions on friends, family, and society.

—Tamiko C., British Columbia

to examine further or simply ignore. There may be times when advice is good, but it's not right for your family at the time or for your child at his particular age. File those pieces of advice in your brain (or in a notebook if you're prone to forget like me) and pull them out later to see if they might work for your family at another season of your homeschooling.

Finally, do what is best for your family. You might decide later to stop using a workbook that everyone else is fond of or find a new music teacher because the drive is too far, but you have to make those decisions based on the needs of your child and your family. In other words, follow your own path.

OUR TRAIL GUIDE

Regardless of the path you choose, fortunately you have a wonderful trail guide. You may remember in chapter 8 that we discussed the navigational systems for life that are available to your children. These include the Holy Spirit, your conscience, godly mentors, books with a biblical worldview, and more. When it comes to help along the path of life—and homeschooling—the Bible (one of our navigational systems) tells us that the Word of God is there to guide us.

Your word is a lamp to my feet and a light for my path. —Psalm 119:105

When we stand at the bottom of a mountain and look at the various trail options, it is very helpful to have those laid out for us.

In addition, along the trail there will sometimes be signs to point us in the right direction, tell how many miles are left, or indicate a dangerous area ahead. These same signs also tell when you've reached the end of the trail. If we didn't have these maps and signs, we might pick any one of the paths and make our way along without help. But we might end up on the wrong path or we might fall off a dangerous overhang that we didn't know about. The freedom to forge up that mountain would be ours nonetheless.

God gave us his Word so that we wouldn't have to stumble along. The path may not always be easy, it may be long, and we may be exhausted by the end of the journey, but we have pointers along the way telling us how to proceed.

FOLLOWING YOUR PATH

As we finish, I hope the following reminders are helpful:

- *Determine why you are homeschooling.* If you do not know why you are doing this, you're likely to become quickly lost on the trails of life. Make a list of the reasons you've decided to homeschool and file that away somewhere so that you can look at it later when you need encouragement or reinforcement.

- *Set goals for your home school.* This is helpful because the goals serve as your finishing point. There have been times when we've set out to hike a trail and we never made it to the end of the trail. We might take a different path or simply turn around and go back. We do eventually end up somewhere, though! And we've always made it home. When you set goals, it doesn't necessarily mean you'll achieve all of them, but at least you have an idea of where you're going.

- *Follow your own path.* Hopefully you'll take a path that is good for your children—without the dense foliage (like changing curriculum ten times in a year) and dangerous cliffs (like intelligence without wisdom) that we mentioned earlier. Many families will change paths during the year because they decide something else is best for their child, just like many families will change curriculum one or two times, but I encourage you to make sure that you still have that lamp unto your feet, the Word of God.

And finally, enjoy the journey! That's a gift unto itself.

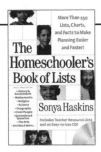

Much more than a reference book, *The Homeschooler's Book of Lists* is filled with facts and essential information that will supplement any elementary-level curriculum. This convenient resource is particularly helpful for teaching multiple grade levels or subjects.

Organized by core academic areas, the lists can be used according to your child's specific needs, learning style, personality, and interests. The book and CD will help you:

- Customize and enrich unit studies
- Encourage memorization work
- Answer questions on the spot
- Spark curiosity in students
- And much more!

With more than 250 lists about great people, important dates, mathematical formulas, word origins, and more—plus special checklists and ideas to aid lesson planning—*The Homeschooler's Book of Lists* is an invaluable tool for home educators and classroom teachers alike.

The Homeschooler's Book of Lists by Sonya Haskins

Print Out Any List From the Easy-to-Use CD!

Best of 2007 (Teacher and Homeschooler Titles) pick from *Exceptional Parent* magazine.